Exploring Manhattan's
MURRAY HILL

Exploring Manhattan's

MURRAY HILL

Alfred Pommer & Joyce Pommer

Charleston THE History PRESS London

Published by The History Press
Charleston, SC 29403
www.historypress.net

Cover images: Original artwork by Sharon Florin.

All maps drawn by Joyce Pommer and Alfred Pommer. All photos taken by Alfred Pommer
unless otherwise indicated.

First published 2013

Manufactured in the United States

ISBN 978.1.62619.059.7

Library of Congress CIP data applied for.

CONTENTS

*Murray Hill's Boundaries and the Murray Hill Historic District's Boundaries
* Story of the Murray Hill Farm (Iclenberg) * Mary Lindley Murray and
the British General Howe * How Murray Hill Got Its Name * Robert Murray
(the Beulah Affair) * Robert Lindley Murray * Development of the Area after
the American Revolution*

A Provocative Sculpture of Christ ** Southeast Corner of East 35th Street and
First Avenue, St. Vartan's Cathedral * Abstract Expressionist Sculpture* Raising
the Cross ** Estonian House (Originally the Civic Club) * Fredrick Norton
Goddard * First View of the Empire State Building * Three Buildings that
Started as Carriage Houses (Malvina Hoffman) * Charles H. Parkhurst *
Stern College for Women, Yeshiva University (Packard Commercial School)*

Contents

Contents

Acknowledgements

The authors would like, once again, to thank our commissioning editor, Whitney Landis, for her expertise and the generous spirit that made working with her a pleasure. And much recognition must also go to the talented and accomplished Sharon Florin for her long hours of hard work in creating the numerous urban landscape paintings that enhance this book, along with its front and back covers.

We would also like to acknowledge our debt to the *AIA Guide of New York*, the *Guide to New York City Landmarks* (New York City Landmarks Preservation Commission) and the many other books—especially those listed in the bibliography—that contributed to making our guidebook possible.

INTRODUCTION

During the American colonial era, the Murray Hill neighborhood was mostly made up of an unsettled area known as Inclenberg, and the area we know today as Murray Hill had its genesis in a large farm built in the 1850s by the Murray family. After the Revolution, the area became developed, with growing numbers of mansions of wealthy New Yorkers. During the Victorian era and by the turn of the twentieth century, retail stores and hotels were moving in, and wealthy New Yorkers were moving northward up Fifth Avenue into Millionaires' Mile. The Murray Hill Farm (Belmont) ran from today's East 34th Street to East 40th Street and from Madison Avenue to Third Avenue. The Murray Hill Neighborhood (postal district) runs from East 27th Street to East 40th Street and from Fifth Avenue to the East River. The Murray Hill Historic District is located along parts of East 35th Street, East 36th Street, East 37th Street and East 38th Street between Lexington Avenue and Park Avenue.

I created this guidebook exploring Murray Hill as a private conversation between me and the reader—a conversation during which I will not only depict the neighborhood through its history and architecture but also discuss some stories that help us understand the mix of people, emotions and ideas—along with the conflicts, compromises and decisions—that took place here, helped shape our nation at its inception and continued throughout its development, all ultimately contributing to our nation's character. This is a tall order for a guidebook, but when we walk across Park Avenue from the south side of East 37th Street and stop on the mall in the middle of Park Avenue, we see a

The shaded areas represent the Murray Hill Hill Historic District
Designated by the New York City Landmarks Preservation Commission

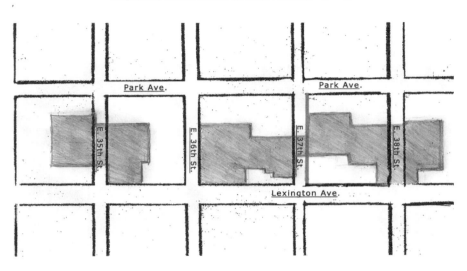

Murray Hill Historic District Map.

stone dedicated to Mary Lindley Murray in 1903, and a plaque placed there installed by the Daughters of the American Revolution reads:

> *This plaque marks the Geographic Center of the Farm known in Revolutionary Days as "Inclenberg," owned by Robert Murray whose wife, Mary Lindley Murray (1726–1782), rendered signal service in the Revolutionary War.*
>
> *Erected by Mary Murray Chapter Daughters of the American Revolution 1926. Replaced by the Murray Hill Committee 1994.*

The "signal service" refers to the tale of Mary Lindley Murray entertaining General Howe and his officers until General Putman and his troops could escape. This is a story that deals with patriotism, deceit, military conflict, domestic conflict, confrontation, compromise and religion.

Another of my stories tells of a different type of confrontation and compromise, one that occurred about 130 years later only a few blocks from

Mary Lindley Murray plaque, 37th Street and Park Avenue.

this site, at J.P. Morgan's mansion. Morgan gathered groups of commercial bankers and trust company presidents and locked them in his mansion for days until they reached an agreement about contributing to a $25 million pool to protect a number of weaker trusts during the financial crisis of 1907. This was a dramatic example of how J.P. Morgan orchestrated a number of thrilling rescues during the financial crisis of 1907. Within two weeks, he had rescued several trust companies and a leading brokerage house and bailed out the City of New York and the New York Stock Exchange. J.P. Morgan's last hurrah made a lasting impression, as America decided that never again should one man wield such power, moving quickly and decidedly toward government financial management (the Federal Reserve System).

I hope you will enjoy my Murray Hill stories, whether you walk through the neighborhood and see each location or decide to read comfortably in your home, allowing my stories and my descriptions of the neighborhood's past and present to stimulate your imagination. Did you know that in 1872, Victoria Woodhull was the first woman to run for president of the United States (on the "Equal Rights" ticket)? Also, Victoria and her sister, Tennessee, were the first women to open a brokerage firm on Wall Street, and they lived in Murray Hill with Victoria's husband, a former husband and her two children. Another interesting Murray Hill story is that Franklin and Eleanor

Roosevelt lived here as newlyweds. I also include some information about such former residents of Murray Hill as Admiral David Farragut ("Damn the torpedoes, full speed ahead"), Dashiell Hammett, Malvina Hoffman, Commodore Matthew C. Perry, Mary Lincoln Isham (Abraham Lincoln's granddaughter) and Delano & Aldrich (architectural firm).

Here is another interesting bit of Murray Hill history: as we pass the site of two Astor mansions, you will find out about the feud between the two Astor families (William Waldorf Astor and his wife, Mary, and William Backhouse Astor Jr. and his wife, Caroline) that gave rise to the first Waldorf Astoria Hotel, which was replaced by the Empire State Building in 1930.

Murray Hill can be deceptive sometimes, giving an impression of architectural blandness. I'm here to tell you that this is not so. If we stop and look, we see some nice postmodern residential skyscrapers along with the iconic Empire State Building. This is all well and good, but what makes the neighborhood really fascinating are the older-styled buildings. I will stop and discuss the historical styles of several surviving former mansions of wealthy New Yorkers, such as the Adelaide L. Townsend Douglas Mansion, the J. Hampton Robb Mansion, the J.P. Morgan Jr. Mansion, the Joseph Raphael De Lamar House and the James F.D. Lanier Mansion, along with some beautifully styled churches from 1854, 1861 and 1868.

You can enjoy this variety from the descriptions, photographs and illustrations in my guidebook or follow the directions to each location and see for yourself. Enjoy your exploration whichever way suits you best.

When I use the phrase "New York City landmark," it refers to the fact that the structure is designated by the New York City Landmarks Preservation Commission as an official New York City landmark. When I state that a structure is a "national landmark," I refer to the fact that the structure is listed on the National Register of Historic Places. Some buildings are both New York City landmarks and national landmarks.

Chapter 1

LOCAL HISTORY

How exactly does the name Murray Hill relate to the part of Manhattan that bears its name? Actually, the Murray Hill name originates from the Battle of Manhattan, which took place in September 1776 during the early stages of the American Revolution on the site of today's Murray Hill neighborhood. At the time, the terrain here was extremely hilly, and Robert and Mary Lindley Murray's farm was located on a hill near what today is East 37th Street and Park Avenue. To this day, a plaque remains at this location commemorating Mary Lindley Murray and her services to her country during the American Revolution.

We can only image the raging internal conflicts that tore at Mary Lindley Murray on September 15, 1776, in the moments after she spied General Howe and his staff walking briskly up the hill toward her front yard. As Mary gathered her three daughters, she remembered herself as a young Quaker girl living in Pennsylvania in 1744, when she met, fell in love with and married Robert Murray, a Scotch American Presbyterian. Mary remembered how easily Robert converted over to the Society of Friends (Quakers), and through her efforts, he gained many very profitable business opportunities by being accepted and included in the social and business networks of the Quaker community. Most of the opportunities involved shipping and overseas trade (imports).

The opportunities and profits that resulted from his involvement with the Quaker networks continued when the Murray family moved to New York in 1753 and took up residence at the corner of Queen (now Pearl) and Wall

Streets—he owned Murray's Wharf at the foot of Wall Street. By 1762, Robert and Mary Murray had purchased a tract of land (Inclenburg) and built a mansion on top of a hill at East 37th Street and Park Avenue that was surrounded by their beautiful twenty-nine-acre country estate (Belmont). The Murrays were doing well and entertained frequently at their country home, where George Washington and other prominent members of New York society were guests.

In the Quaker community, the wife was recognized as an individual with her own political views, and they may well differ from those of her husband. Mary Lindley was known as a fierce Patriot and an unyielding supporter of the American cause. But she soon realized that Robert was an opportunist. Mary must have felt shame when her husband was caught violating the Quaker-led boycott of English goods. Her shame deepened with the Beulah Affair, when he was caught again secretly trading with the English. Robert was shunned in the Quaker community, and it was only through her influence that he regained acceptance.

Obviously, Robert's secret activities were a source of stress and conflict not only between the Quaker community and the Murrays but also between Mary and Robert Murray, as well as between their five grown children—all with mixed, conflicting political views. But the strongest conflict must have been Mary Lindley's internal conflict, fueled by the guilt growing out of her realization that she and her children were enjoying the benefits derived from her husband's secret trading with England. Mary Lindley was dealing with all of these emotions on September 15, 1776, as she led her daughters out their front door to greet General William Howe (a well-known ladies' man). You might say that she was preparing for her most famous party. (This story will be continued in chapter 6.)

The Murray Farm (Inclenberg) was one of a number of farms or country estates on the east side of Manhattan Island. You had John James Duane's Gramercy Seat (now Gramercy Park); James Watts's Rose Hill (now 29th Street and Park Avenue); Beekman's Mount Pleasant (East 50th Street and First Avenue); and, stretching farther north, the mansions (country estates) of the Schermerhorns, the Rhinelanders, the Lawrences and others.

Even though some of these estates grew crops for profit and provided refuge from epidemics, one could argue that their primary function was to serve as centers of refinement, especially in the way they emulated the passion for gardening and landscaping that was popular among English estate owners at that time, with their vast lawns, flower beds, greenhouses, fish ponds and so on. Governor Crosby designated Governors Island as his private game preserve, and the De Lancey estate had its own racecourse just off the Bowery where 1ˢᵗ and 2ⁿᵈ Streets are now. During the nineteenth century, most of these country estates were divided into lots and sold, facilitating the growth of Manhattan neighborhoods.

If we look a little more carefully at the events that facilitated the development of the Murray Hill neighborhood, we can understand why this neighborhood retained its residential character more so than any other Midtown area.

In 1831, the New York & Harlem Railroad was incorporated, granting it the right to operate trains over a double track along 4ᵗʰ (Park) Avenue from city hall to the Harlem River (most of the incorporators were associated with Tammany, and many aldermen received blocks of stock as thank-you presents). In 1833, the tracks reached Murray Hill, a valuable piece of property, and a decision was reached to drill a tunnel (still in use) from 33ʳᵈ Street to 40ᵗʰ Street to keep the steam locomotives out of sight in the local neighborhood and ostensibly to level the grade, making it easier for the trains to travel on the hilly terrain. The avenue was renamed Park Avenue, and the tunnel was completed in 1837 with a forty-foot-wide center mall on top. By 1838, you could travel by train from city hall to Harlem for twenty-five cents, but as you passed under the Murray Hill neighborhood, the noise and dirt from the steam locomotives were not visible from the street. To this day, the tunnel is still there and is now used to divert automobile traffic from that section of Park Avenue.

After the Revolution, Mary Lindley Murray died in 1780 and Robert Murray in 1786. Robert and Mary Lindley Murray had leased the land for the Murray Hill Farm from the municipality in about 1761. The land (twenty-nine acres) was purchased outright by their descendants in 1799, and it was their descendants who, in the 1840s, had the "Murray Hill Restrictive Agreement" inserted into each deed as the Murray Hill property was being divided into building lots and sold. The agreement provided that the lots could be used for residential purposes only, barring businesses and commerce from the neighborhood. Over the decades, this provision, still in the many deeds sold by Murray descendants, was a strong factor in keeping the Murray Hill neighborhood the most residential of all the Midtown neighborhoods.

During the second half of the nineteenth century, Murray Hill became one of the prime neighborhoods in Manhattan's Gilded Age as wealthy New Yorkers (William Waldorf Astor, William Backhouse Astor Jr., J.P. Morgan, Samuel P. Sarsaparilla Townsend, Alexander T. Steward, Joseph R. De

Lamar, J.H. Robb, Theodore Havemeyer, Alfrederick Smith Hatch, Adelaide L. Townsend Douglas, William R. Grace, James and Sara Roosevelt and many others) flocked into Murray Hill. In 1892, when Mrs. Caroline Astor held her last Murray Hill ball, the social register listed the names of more than one hundred Murray Hill residences.

As the Gilded Age faded and the turn of the last century passed into history, the original landed gentry moved northward, leaving behind the Morgan partners and other great financiers, as well as some of the early shipping families. In 1903, B. Altman built his department store between Fifth Avenue and Madison Avenue and between 34th and 35th Streets, one square block, at the very center of elegant Murray Hill. Within a few years, W. & J. Sloane, Arnold Constable & Company and Bergdorf Goodman followed on Fifth Avenue, along with Tiffany's. Fifth Avenue was transformed from a street lined with townhouses and mansions to a world-renowned commercial boulevard.

The Murray Hill neighborhood became increasingly middle class (or upper-middle class) and commercial. Mansions were replaced by apartment buildings or were turned into multifamily dwellings. The southwest corner of West 34th Street and Fifth Avenue seems to represent the neighborhood's evolution. In the mid-nineteenth century, there were two Astor mansions on Fifth Avenue between 33rd and 34th Streets. By 1895, they had been replaced by the first Waldorf Astoria Hotel, and by 1930, the hotel had, in turn, been replaced by the Empire State Building.

The Murray Hill Restriction of 1847 had served the neighborhood well, from Madison Avenue going east (Madison Avenue was the western border for the Murray Farm). Although challenged many times up to the highest courts, the restriction was upheld (east of Madison Avenue) with few exceptions. But one thing that the Murray descendants could not have foreseen was a new type of "dwelling": the apartment house. In 1920, the home of the late Charles T. Barney (of Knickerbocker Trust fame), at the northeast corner of Park Avenue and 38th Street, was replaced by Murray Hill's first apartment house (fifteen stories). Then, Judge Russell's house (southeast corner of Park Avenue and 37th Street) was replaced by a co-operative apartment building in 1922.

The Murray Hill Association could not prevent the rise of the apartment houses along the avenues of the neighborhood, but it could—and did— use the 1847 restriction to prevent the conversion of entire buildings for commercial use and to block wholesale demolition of buildings and the consolidation of lots for the building of large office spaces.

Between the two world wars and on into the postwar period, Murray Hill underwent many physical changes, but its residential character remained. In 1960, the city proposed a drastic widening of 36th and 37th Streets to enable an increased flow of traffic in and out of the Midtown Tunnel. The Murray Hill Committee (now the Murray Hill Neighborhood Association) rallied successfully to save the stoops and front sidewalks of the townhouses. In the mid-1980s, the committee stopped the Community Church from demolishing a row of townhouses along 35th Street to build a high-rise tower. The result was a restriction on all high-rise buildings on the side streets of Murray Hill between Madison and Third Avenues. Another way the preservation fight continues is by having buildings in the neighborhood landmarked. So far, such efforts have resulted in the designation of ten New York City landmarks in Murray Hill and the creation of the official Murray Hill Historic District.

The neighborhood always seemed to retain a large number of older, wealthy residents, but as the twenty-first century approached, a number of high-rise condominiums were built, including the Manhattan Place Condominiums in 1984, the Whitney in 1986, the Corinthian in 1987 and the Horizon in 1988.

If you walk the side streets of Murray Hill as you read this guidebook, you can easily imagine the neighborhood that existed here more than one hundred years ago. Murray Hill is a unique Manhattan neighborhood with more history that we can imagine, and remnants for its past are there if you know where to look. If you remember those one hundred Murray Hill residences that I mentioned that were listed in the social register of 1892, well, dozens of the buildings are still standing intact. Murray Hill is now, as it was then, a unique residential enclave in Midtown Manhattan.

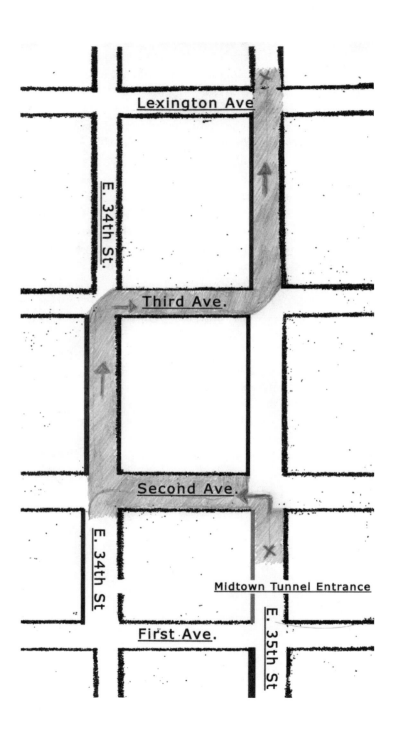

Chapter 2

OUR TOUR BEGINS

*Second Avenue, East 35th Street, East 34th Street and East 35th
Street Between Third Avenue and Lexington*

As we travel through the Murray Hill neighborhood, you will notice that it can be separated into two areas: the original Murray Hill area (the land that was the Murray Farm, 34th Street to 40th Street and Third Avenue to Madison Avenue)—the area that was affected by the Murray Hill Restrictive Agreement—and the expanded Murray Hill neighborhood, which evolved around that immediate area and is defined now as the Murray Hill Postal District (27th Street to 40th Street and Fifth Avenue to the East River).

Let's start the walk on the **southeast corner of East 35th Street and Second Avenue**. If we look up in a northeast direction, we can see the Corinthian apartment building (condominiums). It is located between 37th Street and 38th Street between First and Second Avenue on the site of the former two-story Eastern Airlines Terminal Building, which opened in 1953 and for thirty years provided bus links for millions of travelers to Kennedy International and LaGuardia Airports. It closed in 1984 and was sold by the Metropolitan Transit Authority (MTA) to developers (Bernard Spitzer, Peter L. Malkin and two other corporations) in 1985.

The Corinthian, a fifty-five-story tower that opened in 1988, was designed by architect Michael Schimenti and design architect Der Scutt. It is an excellent example of the International Style II, which is a modern style that plays more freely with shapes and structures than the earlier Modernist buildings produced by the International Style. The International Style II includes a wider variety of designs (such as cylindrical buildings, sloping roofs and unusual shapes).

Statue *Christ* on a wall of St. Vartan.

After viewing the Corinthian, if we simply turn around, we will start to realize that there is a sharp contrast of historical and anti-historical styles even within the expanded area that evolved around the original Murray Hill Farm. We are standing by the rear wall of St. Vartan Armenian Cathedral, and when we walk about one hundred feet east on 35th Street, we will see a provocative, hand-carved, eighteen-foot-tall (with pedestal) limestone statue, *Christ*, mounted on the wall above East 35th Street. It is provocative because most New Yorkers who pass the statue would be quite surprised to learn that it was a statue representing Jesus Christ.

The sculptor, Koren Der Harootian (1909–1992), depicts Christ vulnerable, slightly clothed and with a crown of thorns. The statue is oversize life, but the face is not recognizable to most non-Armenian Christians as that of Jesus Christ, and the crown of thorns also may not be perceived as such. Der Harootian was an Armenian American artist, sculptor and painter. In 1915, when he was six years old, Der Harootian witnessed the persecution and massacre of Armenians by Turks, including the murder of his father, who was a priest.

Koren Der Harootian. *Ink drawing on paper by Sharon Florin.*

He fled with his mother and sister to Russia and ultimately arrived in the United States in 1921. They settled in Worcester, Massachusetts, and he studied at Worcester Art Museum School and at the National Academy of Fine Arts in New York. By 1944, he had moved to New York permanently, and in 1946, he was living in Murray Hill with his English wife in a small apartment with a two-burner gas plate in an old building at 245 East 27th Street. The building had a courtyard that he used to create his stone sculptures.

Der Harootian favored classical and religious subjects (such as for *David and Goliath* and *Orpheus and Eurydice*) as metaphors for the fears, violence and conflicts of World War II. His works display his social conscience in dealing with allegorical and biblical themes and focus on generalizations that provoke primitive symbolic feelings rather than individualized realism.

Koren Der Harootian's works included a 780-pound marble sculpture in 1948, *Prometheus and Vulture*, which is now part of the permanent collection of the Metropolitan Museum of Art in New York City. Also,

Descent from the Cross sculpture.

the 1955 marble statue *Anhid*, a pagan goddess, was exhibited at the Guggenheim Museum.

Now, if we return to Second Avenue and walk toward 34th Street, we can enter the front courtyard of the church and examine a bronze, ten-foot-high abstract expressionist sculpture, *Descent from the Cross*, dedicated on November 11, 1977, and created by sculptor Ruben Nakian (1897–1986). The sculpture is a construction of lunging and leaning elements (large textured blocks, aligned vertically and diagonally, that appear to be tumbling downward). Nakian said in a interview with *New York Times* critic Grace Glueck that he was inspired by Peter Paul Rubens's painting *Raising the Cross*.

Nakian, an American sculptor (Armenian parents), was trained in the classical tradition. His abstract works were inspired by Renaissance and Baroque masters. Nakian explored heroic themes that he infused with raw expressionist energy, as he did with *Descent from the Cross*. Nakian has seven sculptures and two drawings that are part of the permanent collection of the Metropolitan Museum of Art, including *Europa and the Bull with Cupid* (1948), *Satyr* (1950), *Leda and the Swan* (1959) and *Garden of the Gods* (1980).

While standing in the front courtyard, we can see a design above the door that depicts St. Vartan, the Brave. On the door, the image on the right shows St. Vartan receiving a blessing, and the image on the left shows his military nature (helmet at the foot) as well as his peaceful nature (the animal). Vartan Mamigonian was an Armenian who lived during the fourth century and is remembered for his martyrdom at the Battle of Avarayr in AD 451 between Armenian and Iranian forces in present-day Albania. Vartan, his companion Levon (St. Ghevont) and their comrades suffered a military defeat in which they all were killed. They lost the battle but not the war, as both fought and died for their Christian faith, and both became martyrs and saints. It is believed that they ultimately determined the fate of Armenia. Vartan (St. Vartan Mamigonian) and Levon (St. Ghevont) became two of the most beloved of all Armenian saints. The Persians eventually stopped their attempts to convert the Armenians to their religion (Zoroastrianism).

We can get a nice view of the cathedral by walking to the southeast corner of East 34th Street and Second Avenue. St. Vartan Armenian Cathedral opened in 1967. It is the first cathedral of the Armenian Apostolic Church constructed in North America and the headquarters of the Diocese of the Armenian Church of America. The complex includes the chapel, the bookstore and a cultural/religious center, and a museum is planned. The complex was designed by Walker O. Cain of Steinman and Cain as a limestone version of the many early cruciform Romanesque Armenian churches found in Asia Minor. The two notable architectural features of the cathedral are the crucifix dovetailing (with crosses rising vertically) on the corners of the cathedral and the twenty-three-karat-gold leaf dome roof (it replaced the fourteen-karat-gold leafing in 1999). St. Vartan was one of the first churches in North America to use cruciform, dovetailed crosses as a symbolic decoration on its façade.

Now, as we walk along East 34th Street toward Third Avenue, we will stop in front of **243 East 34th Street**, the Estonian House (since 1946). The house was originally built as the Beaux Art–style Civic Club in 1898–99. The clubhouse was commissioned by a local social reformer, Fredrick Norton Goddard (1861–1905), for the purpose of helping the poor by reducing poverty and fighting against gambling (numbers).

The handsome, four-story limestone and brick clubhouse was designed by the Brooklyn architect Thomas A. Gray with a façade that is enriched by a variety of decorative details and distinguished by a rusticated ground floor with a rounded, arched doorway and two large, rounded, arched windows. The second floor features a bow central window with two French doors. On top of the third floor is a modillioned roof cornice under a stone balustrade and a steep-pitched copper mansard roof.

The Civic Club is a New York City and a national landmark. When Fredrick Norton Goddard died of a brain hemorrhage at forty-four years old, the Civic Club closed to honor his passing, and the city lost a remarkable civic leader. To understand what kind of person Fredrick Goddard was, we need to remember that he lived during what is now referred to as the Gilded Age, an age of extreme extravagance and wealth. Fredrick was an idealistic but unhappy young man who was born into a wealthy family, raised in luxury, graduated from Harvard in 1882 and immediately joined his father's dry goods business, J.W. Goddard & Sons, at 100 Bleecker Street. When his father died, Fredrick and his brother, Warren, inherited a fortune worth about $12 million. Shortly after his father's death, Fredrick left his family, his associates and his friends and abandoned his social environment by renting one floor of a tenement at 327 East 23rd Street, where he lived with one old trusted servant.

According to Fredrick Goddard, he did not go into the tenement district with the idea of doing good or helping others. He just wanted to leave a life that he had found troublesome, one that had separated him from the real world. Fredrick sought a new environment so that he could live closer to that real world—closer to the life that most people live, as compared to that of his former friends and associates, whom he felt existed in their own protected,

The Civic Club (now Estonian House).

privileged world. In other words, he had a strong desire to become a part of the poor, working-class tenement community by sharing their problems, their confidences, their sorrows and their pleasures—not to pity them or to exploit them.

Fredrick's purposes shifted slightly early on when he met and made friends with a small group of about twelve sincere, hardworking men (the group included a ferryboat worker, a bricklayer, a plasterer and other workers). The workers had frequent meetings near Fredrick's tenement apartment for the purpose of developing themselves by studying how to improve the conditions and lives of others in their neighborhood. Initially, Fredrick was an outsider, but in a short time, working closely with the workers, he became the group's heart and soul, as well as its leader. The little group grew and took the name of the Civic Club. From the start, an important part of the self-imposed duties of its members was to give personal service, as well as pecuniary aid, to anyone needing it within their perceived district (Fourth Avenue to the East River and East 23rd Street to East 42nd Street).

In 1899, Fredrick Goddard married Miss Alice S. Winthrop, a socialite, and moved to a townhouse at 273 Lexington Avenue. He continued his activities at the Civic Club and expanded them to include a campaign

The Empire State Building.

against the policy game (numbers), and he founded the Anti-Policy Society, which eventually realized the triumph of passing the anti-policy law of 1901. He also worked toward the arrest and conviction of the infamous "policy king" Al Adams in the same year. Fredrick Goddard's political career grew as he founded the East Side Republican Club at 217 East 34th Street. He was elected district leader of the Twentieth District and served for five years, during which he revolutionized the political methods within the district.

When Fredrick Goddard died in 1905, the Civic Club declined, and the building was sold in 1946 by Alice S. Winthrop Goddard to the Estonian Educational Society, which now serves as an educational and cultural center for Estonians in New York City.

We will now walk to the northwest corner of East 34th Street and Third Avenue and look west for a nice view of the Empire State Building. If we had been standing on this corner on Saturday, July 18, 1945, at 9:50 a.m., we would have heard a loud noise: U.S. army pilot William B. Smith received the shock of his life as he crashed his B-25 Bomber into the seventy-ninth floor (room 7915) of the Empire State building.

Smith was building up flying hours (practice miles) needed for a war assignment. He left from Bedford Field near Boston. When Smith reached New York, he was lost in a heavy fog and flew smack into the building, killing eleven Catholic war relief workers who were instantly burned in a white flash while still seated at their desks (one of the workers was found seated at his desk with a pen in his hand, and another worker had a notebook in his lap).

There were 1,500 people in the building, far fewer than on a regular weekday. One woman, Betty Low Oliver, was on an elevator when the plane hit, and the elevator's cable snapped, causing the elevator to drop eighty floors. However, she survived! When the plane hit the building's north (34th Street) façade at the seventy-ninth floor, its engine broke loose of the plane and slid across the long, empty hallway, crashing through its south (33rd Street) façade and landing a block away on an apartment building's roof. The Empire State Building swayed fiercely, and bits of the building fell to earth. There was no structural damage to the building, but the crash left a hole about forty feet in diameter, in the façade. The tragedy took a total of thirteen lives, including that of the pilot and the copilot.

350 Fifth Avenue, the Empire State Building, is a New York City (exterior and the ground-floor lobby) and a national landmark. It was built from 1929 to 1931, with 102 floors, it is 1,250 feet high and it was the tallest building in the world from 1931 to 1973. The Empire State Building was commissioned by John J. Raskob (vice-president of General Motors) and designed by William Lamb of Shreve, Lamb & Harmon. Initially, the Empire State building was to be about 70 stories high until Raskob learned that Walter Chrysler had hired William Van Alen to design the Chrysler Building as the world's tallest building (it was for eleven months). Raskob said that he would not let Chrysler outdo General Motors and filed new plans with the city, increasing the height of the Empire State Building to make sure that it was the tallest building in the world when completed. Raskob named Alfred E. Smith (four-time governor of New York and, in 1929, the first Catholic candidate for the presidency of the United States) as president of the Empire State Building in 1931. The façade has a minimum amount of Art Deco ornament and is limestone, granite, nickel and aluminum.

From here, we walk on Third Avenue to East 35th Street and make a left turn to three buildings (159, 157 and 155 East 35th Street) that were originally built as carriage houses (stables). There is a plaque on 157 East 35th Street that notes that Malvina Hoffman (1887–1966) died here. She worked and lived here from 1914 to 1966 (fifty-two years). Hoffman was a student of

Above: Three former carriage houses: 157, 155 and 153 East 35th Street.

Left: Malvina Hoffman. *Ink drawing on paper by Sharon Florin.*

Rodin, a sculptor and author. She was well known for her many life-size bronze sculptures of people and also worked in marble and plaster. Hoffman is best remembered for her series of 101 portraits, "Races of Mankind"—including busts, full-length figures of individuals and small family groups—life-size statues of members of diverse cultural groups that she created for the Field Museum of Natural History in Chicago Illinois, as a result of her anthropological study trip around the world.

Now we will walk about a quarter of a block west to 133 East 35th Street, the site of the home of Reverend Charles Parkhurst (1842–1933) from 1880 to 1918. Parkhurst was the pastor of the Madison Square Presbyterian Church at East 24th Street and Madison Avenue and a leader in the Social Gospel movement. He was appointed president of the Society for the Prevention of Crime in 1891.

Parkhurst was more than fifty years old and had been a pastor of the church for more than ten years when on Sunday, February 14 (Valentine's Day) in 1892, he decided to give a blistering sermon. In no uncertain terms, Parkhurst accused New York City district attorney De Lancey Nicoll (who lived at 123 East 38th Street in Murray Hill) of being part of a corrupt Tammany Hall administration in league with the owners of the city's vice resorts. Parkhurst thundered on about police brutality and how the corrupt city administration fed on the city's population while pretending to protect it. Parkhurst continued about Tammany Hall: "While we fight iniquity, they shield and patronize it; while we try to convert criminals, they manufacture them." In another part of the same speech, Parkhurst alluded to Tammany Hall as a "form under which the devil disguises himself." After the sermon, Parkhurst was called to testify before a municipal grand jury but could not produce either proof or a substantial record of his allegations. No charges were brought against anyone.

Parkhurst was not deterred. He hired a detective to take him to the city's most reprehensible locations where deplorable criminal activity (mostly prostitution, drugs, pedophilia and worse) could be found operating in the open. Times, places and activities were documented and witnessed (with signed affidavits).

During one episode, Parkhurst got involved in some genial banter with a small group of prostitutes. He actually joined them in a friendly street game of "Johnny Ride a Pony." He was unpleasantly surprised the next day when he saw his picture in the newspapers, actively playing the game with the ladies. The joke was on him, and a lot of cracks were made about the incident, but again, Parkhurst was not deterred. His campaign against police brutality

Reverend Charles H. Parkhurst. *Ink drawing on paper by Sharon Florin.*

and corruption continued—more sermons, hiring detectives and more going undercover to gather information about saloons, brothels and gambling dens, as well as more affidavits.

On March 13, 1892, he preached another sermon, this time backed with the documentation. Parkhurst exposed dishonest politicians not only in sermons but also in court testimony. Finally, when the reform committees and the reforms started, they came one after another. The Lexow & Mazet investigation focused on police corruption and brutality. The Committee of 15 tried to stop prostitution. The William T. Jerome investigation focused on gambling. Parkhurst is credited with bringing about the election of William I. Strong as a reform mayor in 1894 and the appointment of Theodore Roosevelt as chairman of the police board in 1895.

All of this was good, but it actually sounds better than it was because these reforms had a temporary effect—mostly they focused on putting the small offenders on the streets in jail but leaving the network of corrupt police, politicians and underworld people untouched. Those people adapted, and some even benefited because the reform campaigns tended to put the small-time operations out of business, putting the concentration of power in a few politically connected hands. Prohibition tended to exaggerate the condition, as was demonstrated by the Seabury Committee, the largest probe up to that time. It brought down Jimmy Walker's administration in 1933 and found ties to politicians and the police department deeper than they had been in the 1890s. The problems just got worse. The earlier reforms were more like bandages that do not deal with the source of a sickness but merely treat its symptoms.

As we pass by the southeast corner of East 35th Street and Lexington Avenue, we notice the Stern College for Women, Yeshiva University at **253 Lexington Avenue**. Founded in 1954, the college was a pioneer in the field

Stern College for Woman (Packard Commercial School).

of women's education, offering women the opportunity to earn bachelor's degrees in the arts and sciences and immerse themselves in rigorous Jewish studies at the same time and in the same place.

The building was built in 1911 and opened as the Packard Commercial School in 1912; by 1954, the school had closed. The school was commissioned by the widow of Silas S. Packard (the school's founder) and designed by architect H.F. Ballantyne as a modern adaptation of the Georgian (Colonial) style that conveyed a dignity befitting the school it housed. The building achieves monumentality with its impressive brick pilasters on East 35th Street and the engaged brick columns on Lexington Avenue. Its rusticated limestone ground floor, with the many rounded arch openings, was described by Ballantyne as a massive arcade, providing support to the columns above and space for street-level stores (meant to provide additional income).

When the attractive school building opened in 1912, it was an embellishment among the stately structures of the surviving Murray Hill neighborhood. However, it also foreshadowed the commercial development that was to integrate into the very heart of the Murray Hill neighborhood.

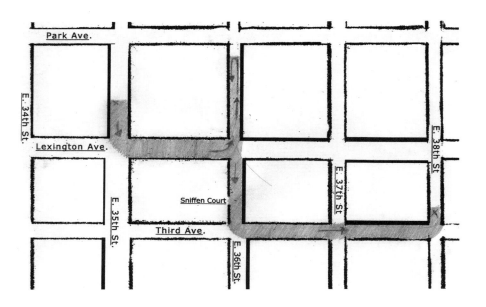

Park Ave.

E. 34th St.

Lexington Ave.

E. 35th St.

Sniffen Court

Third Ave.

E. 36th St.

E. 37th St.

E. 38th St.

Chapter 3

ENTERING THE MURRAY HILL
HISTORIC DISTRICT

*Lexington Avenue, East 35ᵗʰ Street, East 36ᵗʰ Street
and East 38ᵗʰ Street*

If we continue walking west on East 35ᵗʰ Street across Lexington Avenue, we will enter the **Murray Hill Historic District**, which consists of a mix of old brownstones, a mansion, an Art Moderne apartment building and various other elements that come together between Lexington Avenue and Park Avenue on parts of East 35ᵗʰ Street, East 36ᵗʰ Street, East 37ᵗʰ Street and East 38ᵗʰ Street.

Only in Manhattan—I find it amazing that in an area no larger than a few square blocks, we can find a history of so many people who contributed so much to our American culture and history in any number of ways, and each at different points in time. The idea that they were not related to one another in any way, other than the fact that at some point they lived on the same block or within a few blocks of one another, seems extraordinary and is the reason for my guidebook and my walking tours.

In the following chapters, you will find out that Commodore Perry lived on East 36ᵗʰ Street, and several years after he died, Admiral Farragut moved into the house next door. About thirty years later, Franklin and Eleanor Roosevelt (newly wed) moved into a brownstone just five or six doorways down on the same block. Two blocks north, John Quincy Adams Ward (the celebrated American sculptor) lived on East 38ᵗʰ Street in 1870; several doors away from him, the studio of Delano & Aldrich (influential architectural firm at the turn of the last century) opened in 1907, and one of the firm's founders, Aldrich, also lived on the same block. One of Abraham Lincoln's granddaughters had her home across the street (on the same block). And F.

Number 123 East 35th Street, J.F.D. Lanier Mansion.

Scott Fitzgerald stayed at a hotel on the next block. You'll notice during the tour that this phenomenon continues, on and on.

We will next stop in front of **123 East 35th Street**. This five-story mansion survives as a symbol of the Murray Hill lifestyle during the Gilded Age. It was built between 1901 and 1903 as the mansion of James F.D. and Harriet Lanier, and it replaced two older brownstones. The surviving mansion is a New York City landmark and a national landmark—five stories high and 33 feet wide, with 14,160 square feet of interior floor space.

This Beaux Arts–style mansion reflects the principles and influence of the French design style that was popular for fashionable residential architecture in Murray Hill and other wealthy New York city neighborhoods during the Gilded Age. The Beaux Arts design elements that stand out include its rusticated stone base and three ground-floor, round, arched openings (the doorway and two windows) and a bull's-eye window over the entrance that features a set of carved wood paneled doors flanked by cornucopia (a horn containing food and drink, symbolizing abundance)—quite appropriate for this Gilded Age Murray Hill mansion. Also, there is a paneled newel post topped with stone urns that intersects both a stone balustrade and a wrought-iron fence. On the second floor, we see French doors and colossal

Ionic pilasters that separate the bays on the second and third floors. The third floor has projecting sills and a central keystone. On the top floor, we find a lacy wrought-iron balustrade topped with a copper mansard roof and three pedimented dormers. All together, it is an elegant and dignified design that would fit comfortably either in New York or Paris at the turn of the last century.

Designed by architects Hopper and Koen (who studied at the École des Beaux-Arts in Paris, France, and worked with McKim, Mead & White before going out on their own) for James Franklin Doughty Lanier (1858–1928), who along with his wife, Harriet Bishop (1866–1931), and other members of their families had been Murray Hill residents for decades. James F.D. Lanier was a banker associated with Winslow, Lanier & Company, a firm founded by his grandfather. He also was an avid sportsman, a founder of the Meadowbrook Hunt Club and a pioneer automobile driver in touring and racing. Lanier married Harriet Bishop in 1885, and they had two sons. James F.D. Lanier was the son of Charles Lanier (1836–1926), who was a banker for sixty-three years (Winslow, Lanier & Company) and a very close friend of J.P. Morgan Sr. Charles was a member of a small group called the Corsair Club, which made its headquarters on Morgan's yacht. Charles Lanier was treasurer of the Hospital Saturday and Sunday Association, a forerunner of the United Hospital Fund.

Harriet Lanier founded (in 1913) and served as president for the Society of Friends of Music, organized for the purpose of bringing to the public's attention "rare and little-known works, old and of today." The society had its own chorus under the leadership of Arthur Bodanzky.

Directly across East 35th Street from the Lanier mansion, we find **112 East 35th Street**, the New York New Church, built in 1858 (serving New York since 1812). The church is also called the Church of New Jerusalem (sometimes described as Swedenborgian) and has a total of thirty-one congregations in the United States and seven in Canada. The church espouses a Christian faith based on the spiritual teaching of Emanuel Swedenborg (1688–1772), who believed that "all people, who live good lives, no matter what their religion have a place in heaven." The church is designed as a modest Renaissance Revival complex—its front garden gives a spatial break to the block.

Members of the New Church came to the United States in the 1790s and lived and worshiped in Lower Manhattan. The church received the property in Murray Hill in 1853, and by 1859, the church was completed and the congregation had become a part of the Murray Hill neighborhood.

Number 112 East 35th Street, New York New Church.

Here are a few interesting side notes about the church. President Thomas Jefferson had John Hardgrove, a member of the Swedenborgian congregation in Baltimore, preach in the Capitol before Congress. John Chapman, also known as "Johnny Appleseed," besides his legendary activity sowing seeds in the Midwest, carried with him Swedenborgian publications and distributed them where and when he could. Among the New Church's many prominent New York members were Henry James (author), William Seward (governor of New York, U.S. senator and secretary of state under Lincoln), Walt Whitman (poet), John Bigelow, George Inness and Lois Burnham Wilson. The first minister of the New York New Church in 1859 was Professor George Bush, who was a first cousin, four times removed, to President George Herbert W. Bush.

Let's leave the New York New Church and walk around the corner to **125 East 36th Street**, a former home to Franklin and Eleanor Roosevelt from 1905, when they returned from a European honeymoon, to 1908, when they moved into a mansion at 47 East 65th Street that was a part of a larger double mansion built by Franklin's mother, Sara, who was living in the adjacent mansion at 49 East 65th Street.

Franklin married Eleanor (a fifth cousin four times removed) in 1905 in spite of his mother's strong objections, and Franklin broke a longstanding

Franklin and Eleanor Roosevelt in Hyde Park, New York, 1906, on vacation. *Courtesy of the Franklin Roosevelt Presidential Library and Museum.*

Roosevelt family tradition (of being closely associated with the Republican Party) by joining the Democratic Party in 1908.

While Franklin was living at 125 East 36th Street with Eleanor, he was working as a corporate lawyer in Manhattan and living a typical upper-class life. They had two children while living at 125 East 36th Street: Anna, born in 1906, and James, born in 1907. In 1908, bored with his work, Franklin decided to enter politics. You might say that he was moving up in the world, moving to the Upper East Side's Millionaires' Mile neighborhood in 1908, getting elected as New York State senator in 1910 and again in 1912, being appointed assistant secretary of the navy by President Woodrow Wilson in 1913, being elected governor of New York in 1928 and again in 1930 and then finally moving up to the United States presidency. Basically, Franklin followed the same path traveled by his distant cousin, Theodore Roosevelt— only Teddy was a Republican.

In 1920, Franklin Roosevelt ran as the candidate for vice president on the Democratic ticket, with James M. Cox running for president. They lost the election. About a year later, in the summer of 1921, while on vacation with his family at their summer home on Campobello Island, off the coast of Maine, Franklin felt weak and went to bed early—he woke up early the next day with a high fever and a weakness in his legs. By the following day, he could no longer stand. He was diagnosed with polio (it probably was Guillain-Barré syndrome).

Without the use of his legs, Franklin increased his upper-body strength with exercise. Soon he was able to move himself in and out of bed and his wheelchair, as well as up stairs. He had special hand controls installed in his car so he could drive.

Franklin D. Roosevelt (1882–1945) was the only United States president elected four times (1932 to 1945). He led America through the Great Depression (expanding the role of the federal government with a number of programs and reforms referred to as the "New Deal") and World War II. Eleanor Roosevelt (1884–1962) was the longest-serving First Lady of the United States, holding the post from 1933 to 1945 during Franklin D. Roosevelt's four terms in office. President Harry S Truman nicknamed her the "First Lady of the World" in tribute to her human rights achievements.

Eleanor was born into a wealthy, well-connected New York family, the Roosevelts. She had an unhappy childhood, with the deaths of both parents and one of her brothers by the age of ten. Eleanor attended Allenwood Academy in London and was deeply influenced by feminist headmistress Marie Souvestre. After returning to the United States, she married her distant cousin, Franklin D. Roosevelt. Eleanor's marriage was complicated from the beginning by Franklin's controlling mother and more so in 1918 after finding several letters that made it clear that Franklin was having an affair with her secretary, Lucy Mercer. Franklin's mother, Sara, persuaded Eleanor to stay and not divorce Franklin, but Eleanor decided from that time onward to seek fulfillment in a public life of her own. She persuaded Franklin to stay in politics following his partial paralysis from polio in 1921 and began to give speeches and campaign in his place. After Franklin's election as governor of New York, Eleanor regularly made public appearances on his behalf.

When Franklin became president in 1933, Eleanor dramatically changed the role of the First Lady by making it an important part of American politics. Eleanor gave press conferences and spoke out for human rights, children's causes and women's issues, as well as worked on behalf of the League of Women Voters. She had her own newspaper column, "My Day." Eleanor also spoke and wrote about helping the country's poor and made a stand against racial discrimination. During World War II, she made many trips abroad to visit U.S. troops.

Numbers 113 and 115 East 36th Street, former homes of Admiral Farragut and Commodore Perry.

"The story is over," Eleanor told reporters one day. She said that she did not have any plans to continue her public service after Franklin died, but that is not the way it worked out. Eleanor served from 1945 to 1953 as a delegate to the United Nations General Assembly and became chair of the UN's Human Rights Commission. As a member of the commission, she helped write the Universal Declaration of Human Rights—an effort that she considered to be her greatest achievement. Eleanor wrote several books, including *This Is My Story* (1937), *This I Remember* (1949), *On My Own* (1958) and *Autobiography* (1961).

We can walk a short distance west to **115 East 36th Street**. In 1857, Commodore Matthew Perry (1794–1858) had the townhouse built and moved in. Unfortunately, he was here only about a year before he passed away in 1858 from cirrhosis due to alcoholism. His remains were moved to the Island Cemetery in Newport, Rhode Island, in 1866.

Perry is most remembered as the commodore for the United States Navy who compelled the opening of Japan to the West with the Convention of Kanagawa in 1854. During the Great Depression, this brownstone was converted to a multifamily dwelling with seven apartments, and in 1981, the building turned co-op.

Ironically, the brownstone next door at **113 East 36th Street** was the New York City home of another renowned member of the United States Navy, Admiral David G. Farragut (1801–1870). He led the U.S. Navy during the Civil War. Mobile was the last major Confederate port open on the Gulf of Mexico. The bay was heavily mined (naval mines were known as "torpedoes" then). Farragut gave the order for his fleet to charge the fort. When the monitor USS *Tecumseh* struck a mine and sank, the others started to retreat. Farragut, while lashed to the riggings of his flagship, the USS *Hartford*, shouted through a trumpet, "What's the trouble?" "Torpedoes" was the answer shouted back from USS *Brooklyn*. Farragut answered, "Damn the torpedoes, full speed ahead" and led his fleet to an important victory in the Battle of Mobile Bay (defeating the squadron of Admiral Franklin Buchanan).

New Yorkers heard about Farragut's victory at Mobile Bay, and the famous phrase became a part of our language. In fact, it was actually paraphrased from "Damn the torpedoes!…Four bells. Captain Drayton, go ahead! Jouett, full speed!" Regardless, New Yorkers admired Farragut's brazen courage in the face of danger and adopted him as their hero, and after the war, New York City businessmen took up a collection, totaling about $50,000, to buy Farragut this brownstone in Murray Hill. In 1870, when Farragut died, there was a huge public funeral procession. Thousands stood in a driving rainstorm to watch the coffin as it was carried up Broadway and 5 Avenue to the train that took it to Woodlawn Cemetery for burial. The New York Farragut Association commissioned the Farragut Monument, dedicated in 1881 (designed by Augustus Saint Gaudens and Stanford White, America's first Art Nouveau monument), and it still stands in Madison Square Park.

Now we walk east across Lexington Avenue, leaving the Murray Hill Historic District to pass **Sniffen Court**, a New York City and national historic district—a half-street midway on the south side of East 36th Street between Lexington Avenue and Third Avenue. Here we have a courtyard and ten Romanesque Revival structures built as stables in 1863 and 1864 to serve the mansions of Murray Hill. In the 1920s, the stables were converted to residences at 150 to 158 East 36th Street. Sniffen Court was named for John Sniffen, a local nineteenth-century builder who purchased four standard twenty-five- by one-hundred-foot lots and rearranged them for resale into ten lots with common access to an alley.

Malvina Hoffman (sculptor, author) kept a studio in the rear of the court, where her bas-reliefs of mounted horsemen still flank the front door; there is another entrance and a plaque on East 35th Street. (See the chapter 2 for further details.)

Sniffen Court. *Original oil painting on canvas by Sharon Florin.*

Number 1 Sniffen Court (36th Street) has been owned by the Amateur Comedy Club since 1884. At different points in time, the theater has been known as the Sniffen Court Dramatic Society (an amateur group that performed in full evening dress) and, more recently, as the Murray Hill Comedy Club (four annual performances and a membership of about four hundred members or guests). It is the oldest private theater club in New York City. The building is registered as a legitimate theater, but the theater group has been a private one operated by members and for the amusement of members and their social circle, with no public performances. The group broke with this tradition during World War I when it performed drama for the benefit of members of the military service.

If we look across the street from Sniffen Court at **163 East 36th Street**, we will be looking at the apartment building where the Lunts—Alfred Lunt (1893–1977) and Lynn Fontanne (1887–1983)—had their three-level apartment, with a fireplace, from the 1950s to the early 1960s. They were famous for a long string of hit Broadway plays in which they both starred in together, as well as for the fact that they had a happy marriage that lasted fifty-five years, until he died in 1977.

Lynn Fontanne was born and raised in England, where she started her acting career, and came to the New York in 1910, just twenty-three years old. Alfred Lunt and Lynn Fontanne met in 1919 during a rehearsal at New York's Amsterdam Theater on West 42nd Street; they both had leading roles in Tyler Stock Company's late spring production of *Made for Money*. This was the first time they appeared together on stage but not the last. Alfred married Lynn in 1922, and they went on to perform together twenty-seven times. Alfred Lunt and Lynn Fontanne were the best-loved and most successful acting team in American theatrical history, and with their last performance in 1958, the Globe Theater was renamed the Lunt-Fontanne Theater in their honor.

The Lunts had their country house, Ten Chimneys, at Genesse Depot, Wisconsin, where Alfred enjoyed his two favorite hobbies: cooking and building miniature theaters. They both enjoyed frequent visits from their lifelong friend, Noël Coward. In their long and successful marriage, it seems that Lynn had kept one secret from Alfred, a lie to which she never admitted. When they met, Lynn told Alfred that she was five years younger than him. Actually, she was five years older than him; he died six years before her and never found out about her secret. It seems unlikely that it could have mattered at all to him, but she still insisted until she died in 1983 that she was not born on December 6, 1887, as the birth records in Woodford, London, England, indicate. Somehow, no one knows quite how, she got the Social Security Death Index in the United States to show her birth as December 6, 1893.

We will now walk to Third Avenue and then two blocks to 560 East 38th Street at the southwest corner of Third Avenue. The large apartment building on that corner extends west on East 38th Street, and when we reach just past the rear of the building, we will be looking at the site where a brownstone at 166 East 38th Street was located before 1975. Behind the brownstone that was on this site, there was a stable that was purchased by Gutzon Borglum (1867–1941) in 1901. Borglum remodeled the old stable and made his studio here, which he used until 1912. It was here where Borglum created the plaster model that he used years later as a miniature model for the famous Lincoln head that he created on Mount Rushmore. While working here, Borglum sculpted saints and apostles for the Cathedral of Saint John the Divine, and he had a group sculpture, *The Mares of Diomedes*, accepted by the Metropolitan Museum of Art in 1906. It was the first sculpture by a living American that the museum had ever purchased. Later the same year, the museum accepted Borglum's statue *John Ruskin*. Borglum sold the studio in 1920. Mount Rushmore is located in Pennington County, South Dakota. The faces of the presidents (Theodore Roosevelt, Abraham Lincoln, George Washington and Thomas Jefferson) were completed between 1934 and 1939. Construction on the monument ended in 1941.

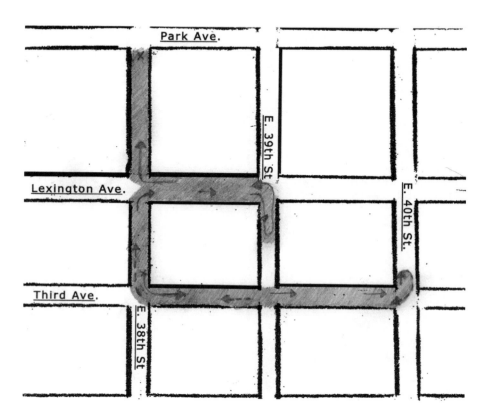

Chapter 4

BOWDOIN STABLE TO THE
TOWNHOUSE APARTMENTS

East 38th Street to East 40th Street Between
Third Avenue and Park Avenue

Across the street at **149 East 38th Street** is the Carriage House Center, which offers elegant space for photo and film shoots, business meetings, seminars, product launches and seated dinners—a venue with an atmosphere of artistry.

The center is housed in a New York City landmark building: the George S. Bowdoin Stable, built in 1902. The brick and stone carriage house was designed by Ralph S. Townsend for William Martin (a large Murray Hill landowner, businessman and real estate developer) in a Renaissance Dutch Revival style. View the façade from the top down to see a semicircular stone pediment topping the stepped gables that rise from a mansard roof; the gable's edges are marked by stone quoins with volutes, and in the center, there is a carved bulldog's head over an oval window with stone surrounds. The second floor includes a stone panel featuring the date the carriage house was built (1902), quoins and splayed lintels. Each end of the spandrel (area below the window) between the first and second floors has a sculptured horse head and a center shield with the building's address over the entrance. The ground floor has three openings (doors), quoins and splayed lintels.

The carriage house was acquired by Bowdoin in 1907, converted to a garage in 1918 by Mrs. Bowdoin and later converted to a single-family residence, eventually yielding to commercial use. The carriage houses remind us that there was a time (the nineteenth century) when horses played a vital part in the city's everyday life, and their care and housing was a necessary part of

Number 149 East 38th Street, Bowdoin Stable.

Number 148 East 40th Street, Jonathan W. Allen Stable.

the city's development. The stables that belong to the wealthy Murray Hill residents were usually kept on a side block, close enough to be convenient but not too near. George S. Bowdoin was a partner in the banking firm of J.P. Morgan and Company and resided in a large house on Park Avenue near East 36th Street, just two blocks from his partner and friend J.P. Morgan Sr. Bowdoin died in 1913, the same year J.P. Morgan Sr. died.

If we walk to Third Avenue, we can make a left two blocks to East 40th Street and then make a left again. There is another landmark stable at **148 East 40th Street**, the Jonathan W. Allen Stable, built in 1871 for Allen, a broker who lived on East 42nd Street. The builder, Charles E. Hadden, designed the brick and stone carriage house in a charming Second Empire style that includes a slate-covered mansard roof; large, rounded head dormers; and delicate iron cresting. The central entrance has historic wood-paneled double doors with glass on the top and which are topped by a segmental brick arch with a stone keystone. There is one smaller door on each side with a glass and wood transom under a round brick arch, and the rest of the decoration combines to create a picturesque carriage house. The two-story carriage house accommodated horses and carriages on the ground floor and had living quarters for the groom on the second floor. Around 1945, the building was converted for commercial use.

Now we will proceed to **152 East 38th Street**, the landmark Gate House, built in 1858 almost directly across from the earlier carriage house. There was a story and a plaque on the front entrance (installed by the New York Landmark Preservation Foundation, a private group) that claimed that it was built as a gatehouse for the estate of a member of President Martin Van Buren's family. But now the plaque is gone because historians believe that this seems unlikely since the estate era in Murray Hill was long gone by 1858. Records show that the house was built by a contractor, Patrick McCafferty, who lived here until he sold the house, and it changed hands a few times until it was sold in 1888 to Mary L. Van Buren, a widow of James Van Buren (occupation unknown). Neither of them was listed as a descendant of President Van Buren in *American President Families*, compiled by Hugh Brogan and Charles Mosely. But the fact that at some point in time a person with the last name of Van Buren did live here may have caused some confusion and given rise to the story.

The house itself is architecturally confusing since it was built in 1858, given a new façade in 1934 and was renovated in 2000, and the New York City landmark designation report is not clear which façade it deems to be the original façade—it seems to keep some elements of the previous façades.

Number 133 East 38th Street, former residence of Dashiell Hammett.

Now we walk a short way toward Lexington Avenue and stop in front of 133 East 38th Street.

In 1931, when Dashiell Hammett (1894–1961) first arrived in Manhattan from California, he rented an apartment at **133 East 38th Street**. He was broke, frustrated with screenwriting and drinking heavily. It was here where he started to write *The Thin Man*, creating the characters Nick and Nora Charles. He soon moved to the Hotel Elsee in Midtown, where he resumed his on-again/off-again lifelong affair with Lillian Hellman. Except for *The Thin Man*, Hammett wrote hardboiled detective novels and short stories that are said to have had a significant influence on film, and he is believed by some to be one of the finest mystery writers of all time. Several enduring characters that Hammett created in his novels include Sam Spade in *The Maltese Falcon*, the Continental Op in *Red Harvest* and *The Daine Curse* and Ned Beaumont in *The Glass Key*. Hammett also wrote dozens of short fiction stories for magazines between 1922 and 1932.

Dashiell Hammett was born on a farm in St. Mary's County in southern Maryland, baptized Catholic and raised in Philadelphia and Baltimore. He left school at thirteen and held several jobs before working as an operative for the Pinkerton National Detective Agency from 1915 to 1922, with time off to serve in World War I in 1918. He served in the Motor Ambulance Corps, contracted tuberculosis and met a nurse, Josephine Dolan; in about a year, they were married. Soon they had two daughters, Mary Jane in 1921 and Josephine in 1926. After the birth of their second child, Josephine was told by Health Services nurses that she and the children should not live with Dashiell full-time because of the tuberculosis. Josephine moved out and rented a home in San Francisco. Hammett would visit on weekends, but the marriage fell apart—he continued to support his wife and daughters with the income he made from his writing.

All of Hammett's characters were based on people he knew or knew about, and his stories were inspired by his experience as a Pinkerton operative—this gave his writing a hardboiled realism that was new to mystery stories up to that time. By 1935, he had stopped writing novels and become involved in left-wing activism. In 1942, Hammett joined the army again, serving as a sergeant in the Aleutian Islands.

After the Second World War, Hammett joined the Civil Rights Congress in 1946. In 1947, the Civil Rights Congress was designated a Communist front group by a presidential executive order. At a court hearing, Hammett invoked his Fifth Amendment right refusing to give names or answer any questions about the congress. He was found guilty of contempt of court and served several months in a West Virginia federal penitentiary. In 1953, he was called to testify before the U.S. Senate Permanent Subcommittee on Investigations (the McCarthy hearings); he refused to cooperate and was blacklisted. Hammett died in 1961 of lung cancer in New York City's Lenox Hill Hospital. He was a veteran of two world wars and was buried at Arlington National Cemetery.

Across the street from Dashiell Hammett's apartment, we can see **128–136 East 38th Street**, built in 1869 as a row of five Italianate-style brownstones. Number 132 East 38th Street was remodeled in 1910; it is four stories, with an English basement, and has more than two thousand square feet of floor space, including a four-hundred-square-foot roof deck. The building is twenty feet wide and twenty-four feet deep. This house was for sale in January 2011 (asking price $2,695,000).

A mildly incongruous story—meant to be ironic in a sense—appeared in the *New York Times* during the winter of 1914. Lawrence Waterbury (1877–1942) was living at 132 East 38th Street as a bachelor and was considered a bit eccentric. One night, in the winter of 1914, the top floor of this townhouse caught on fire as he was dressing for dinner. He casually paused while the fire department put out the blaze and then finished dressing and trotted

Larry Waterbury, member of the undefeated International Polo Team in 1909, 1911 and 1913. *Courtesy of the Library of Congress.*

off to the meal. The reason the story made the newspaper was because Lawrence Waterbury was a polo champion, a ten goaler and a member of the "Big Four," our undefeated international polo team in 1909, 1911 and 1913. His team lost in 1902. The "Big Four" included Harry Payne Whitney, Monte Waterbury, Larry Waterbury and Devereaux Milburn—they helped usher in a new era with an aggressive and fast style of play that defeated/dethroned Great Britain's supremacy in polo. Lawrence Waterbury was the only polo player in the history of the Westchester Cup to have played all four positions. From 1910 to 1914, he won the Westchester Cup and the U.S. Open Championship plus seven Senior Polo titles. Lawrence Waterbury was inducted into the Polo Hall of Fame on March 18, 1993. He was also an uncle by marriage to Eleanor Roosevelt—he married Louise Munn in 1932.

Now we walk around the corner on Lexington Avenue to East 39th Street and make a right turn to **145 East 39th Street**, a New York City landmark hotel that opened in 1919 as the Allerton 39th Street House. The hotel provided quiet, respectable, economical housing for hardworking, ambitious young men and women. The services were provided without the usual restrictions imposed by most residential hotels of the early twentieth century.

Its shared facilities included dining rooms, a reception room for visitors, a library and a solarium off the roof terrace. The athletic facilities included a swimming pool and a gymnasium. The amenities were designed to evoke the exclusivity of "club life." Architect Arthur Loomes Harmon adapted the Northern Italian Renaissance style to the club hotel with strategic use of red terra-cotta details placed above the second-floor windows, balconettes supported by terra-cotta brackets with foliate designs along with Greek and Roman symbols and a rooftop loggia. Harmon emphasized verticality by recessing the window bays. This quickly became the trademark style for the Allerton Club Hotel chain.

In February 1920, F. Scott Fitzgerald (1896–1940) rented a room at the Allerton Hotel. He had returned to New York after a month in New Orleans and had just finished writing *This Side of Paradise*. Upon returning to Manhattan, Fitzgerald tried unsuccessfully to start another novel but settled for writing two of his best-known short stories ("The Jelly Bean" and "May Day") while staying here. It was during his stay at the Allerton Hotel that he and Zelda became engaged. *This Side of Paradise* was published in March, and they were married on April 3, 1920. They had one child, a daughter, Frances Scott Fitzgerald, born in 1921. Between 1920 and 1934, Fitzgerald wrote three more novels: *The Beautiful and the Dammed*, published in 1922; *The Great Gatsby*, published 1925; and *Tender Is the Night*, published in 1934. Fitzgerald died in 1940 from a heart attack while working on his last novel, "The Love of the Last Tycoon." The novel was edited and completed by his friend, the literary critic Edmund Wilson. It was published in 1941 as *The Last Tycoon*.

F. Scott Fitzgerald also had modest financial success as a screenwriter in Hollywood between 1937 and 1940, and over his lifetime, he wrote more than a dozen short stories and essays. F. Scott Fitzgerald died believing himself to be a failure. It wasn't until after his death that he was recognized as an important author in the history of American literature. *The Great Gatsby* can be thought of as the quintessential American novel and as a definitive history of the Jazz Age. F. Scott Fitzgerald not only wrote about the Jazz Age in his stories and novels, but he and Zelda were also living examples of the Jazz Age in the lives they led. Both included their own experiences in their stories.

In 1955, the club hotel was acquired by the Salvation Army and reopened as Ten-Eyck-Troughton Memorial Residence for Women, with supervision and restrictions.

As we walk back to East 38th Street at the northwest corner of Lexington Avenue, we will pass 125 East 38th Street, the Permanent Mission of the

Republic of Benin to the United Nations. And directly across the street, at 315 Lexington Avenue, is the Permanent Mission of Cuba to the United Nations.

We are reentering the official Murray Hill Historic District from Lexington Avenue on East 38th Street, and here there is a row of Italianate-style homes at 136–128 East 38th Street that date from 1869 (no. 134 has been altered).

In 1870, John Quincy Adams Ward (1830–1910), the prominent American sculptor, was living at **134 East 38th Street** as a member of Thomas Boese's household. Boese was a lawyer active in civic affairs, and Ward was the first successful American sculptor educated and trained entirely in the United States—he moved from Ohio to Brooklyn in 1849 to live with his sister and work/train with Henry Kirke Brown for several years. When Ward became the first American sculptor to have his work (*Indian Hunter*) installed in Central Park in 1869, his career flourished. To this day, nine of his works are still on public display in Manhattan, and at least nine more are still displayed across the United States. He is probably most remembered in New York City for his over-life-size standing statue of George Washington on the steps of Federal Hall on Wall Street and for his design *Integrity Protecting the Works of Man* featured in the pediment of the New York Stock Exchange on Broad Street. Ward's work was well known for its realism and artistic excellence.

In 1882, his friend, the prominent American architect Richard Morris Hunt, who collaborated on many projects with Ward over the years, designed a new studio for Ward at 119 West 52nd Street, where Ward lived and worked for many years. J.Q.A. Ward was a trustee of the Metropolitan Museum of Art, a member of the Municipal Art Society and a founder and the first president of the National Sculpture Society.

In 1917, an old stable at **126 East 38th Street** was remodeled into offices for the architectural firm of Delano & Aldrich (more recently used as offices for music publishers). William A. Delano (1874–1960) and Chester H. Aldrich (1871–1940) founded their firm in 1903. They soon became well known for designing mansions and elite private clubs on the Upper East Side, such as the Union Club at 101 East 69th Street (Park Avenue), the Colony Club at 564 Park Avenue (East 62nd Street) and the Knickerbocker Club at 2 East 62nd Street (William A. Delano was a member of the club). The firm helped shape the architectural climate in the United States in the first half of the twentieth century with its originality and creativity in adopting historical styles to notable townhouses, churches, schools, public buildings and country estates. The essence of its creativity lies in the way it combined the functional aesthetic of a Modernist approach with the aesthetic of traditional classical architecture.

One example that illustrates how Delano & Aldrich was able to use historical design elements successfully in modern buildings can be shown in its use of the "Vitruvian Wave," referring to the Roman architect Marcus Vitruvius Pollio, who described the wave in the earliest existing books on Roman architecture during the first century BC. The wave is also described as the "wave scroll" or the "running dog pattern" and resembles a pattern of identical wave tops, running along a band, or a series of scrolls viewed on end. The wave became a signature in classical eighteenth-century English designs and was described as "doing the wave." Delano & Aldrich used the wave successfully in a band over the ground floor entrance of its 1939 Art Moderne–styled Marine Air Terminal at LaGuardia Airport. We can also see the wave in an elite, Federal-styled clubhouse that the firm designed in 1925: the Brook, at 111 East 54th Street, where it used the design in a band over the ground floor.

The adjacent building, at **122–124 East 38th Street**, is a double house designed by Ralph Townsend for Leland H. Martin, who was the head of the men's clothier Roger Peet and also a real estate developer. In 1891, the double house was purchased by Abraham Lincoln's son Richard Todd Lincoln (1843–1926) for his two daughters, Mary ("Mamie," 1869–1938) and Jessie. The double house was later owned exclusively by one of Richard's married daughters and her husband, Mary T. (Lincoln) and Charles Isham.

Mary T. Isham (Lincoln) married Charles Bradford Isham on September 2, 1891, and bought a place in Manchester, Vermont, known as the 1811 House. In 1892, she gave birth to her first and only child, Lincoln Isham, in Manhattan. She lived the rest of her life in Manhattan at 19 East 72nd Street and at 122 East 38th Street (on February 27, 1935, an article in the *Brooklyn Daily* noted that she was living at 122 East 38th Street). Mary was a choir mother of Grace Church on Broadway and East 10th Street. On June 9, 1919, her husband died. Mary continued living in Manhattan until she became gravely ill and died in New York Presbyterian Hospital on November 21, 1938, at about 10:05 a.m. Robert Todd Lincoln, Abraham Lincoln's eldest son, was secretary of war, ambassador to the Court of St. James and president of the Pullman Company.

We now walk about one hundred feet toward Park Avenue and arrive in front of **116 East 38th Street**, the former home of Chester Homes Aldrich, a founding partner in the aforementioned architectural firm Delano & Aldrich. Aldrich lived here with his sister, Amy, and two servants in a house that was part of a row (120–116 East 38th Street) of plain brownstones that were the earliest houses on the block, dating from 1856. Each of the

Numbers 122–124 East 38th Street, double townhouse for Abraham Lincoln's granddaughters.

Number 108 East 38th Street, Townhouse Apartment Building.

brownstones is only fourteen feet wide, and they are joined together by a joint terrace that separates the row from the rest of the block. The plainness and the small front indicate a row of homes initially built for working-class owners; the Italianate brownstones that followed in 1869 were built for more affluent New Yorkers.

We continue walking toward Park Avenue and stop in front of **108 East 38th Street**. The Townhouse opened in 1930, a twenty-two-story luxury apartment building designed by the architectural firm of Bowden & Russell in a moderate Art Moderne style. We see many Art Deco buildings in Manhattan, but the Art Moderne–styled buildings are few and far between. Art Moderne is a subdivision of Art Deco that appeared in Manhattan after the onset of the Great Depression. Although the two styles are sometime mistaken for each other, Art Moderne buildings are usually more austere and streamlined than their Art Deco relatives. Art Moderne didn't have its official coming-out party until the 1937 Paris Exposition. The Townhouse has a dark-red (almost black) brick façade, and the decorative feature that is most visible from the street is the fancy brickwork in the building spandrels beneath the windows. On top is a colorful crown of glazed terra-cotta panels that may be partially visible from the street.

As we walk on East 38th Street to Park Avenue, we are leaving the official Murray Hill Historic District (see map).

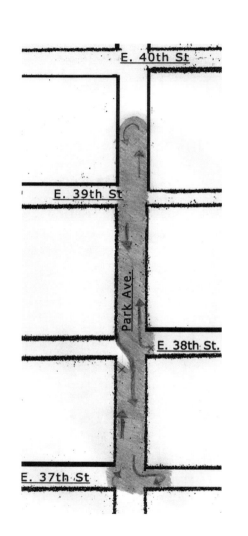

Chapter 5

THE MURRAY HILL HOTEL TO THE
SCANDINAVIA HOUSE

Park Avenue Between East 40ᵗʰ Street and East 37ᵗʰ Street

Now having left the historic district, once we get on Park Avenue and go to **100 Park Avenue** between East 40ᵗʰ Street and 41ˢᵗ Street, we will be where the famous Murray Hill Hotel was built in 1869 and demolished in 1947. It was designed by J.B. Snook, the architect who designed the first Grand Central Station in the 1860s. The public rooms in the hotel had red, white and blue marble floors, fifteen-foot ceilings and elaborate gilt décor. When it opened (and for many years afterward), a night's lodging plus four meals cost four dollars. The hotel was famous for its food and listed seventy-three separate items on the hotel's restaurant breakfast menu. For decades, the hotel had so many regulars that it seemed to operate more like a private club. There was a story in the local newspapers about a woman who was a guest for fifty-three winters.

In 1936, Alf Landon (1887–1997) used the Murray Hill Hotel as his campaign headquarters when he was the Republican candidate for president of the United States in 1936. Landon lost in a landslide. Alf Landon had been elected governor of Kansas in 1932 and was reelected governor in 1934—the only Republican governor in the nation to be reelected that year. As governor, Landon had a reputation for reducing taxes and balancing the budget. Landon was a fiscal conservative who believed that government must address certain social issues, but he also supported parts of the New Deal and labor unions.

Directly across the avenue at 101 Park Avenue is the forty-nine-story, black glass tower designed by Eli Attia and built in 1981. One unusual aspect about

Murray Hill Hotel 1910 on Park Avenue between East 40ᵗʰ Street and East 41ˢᵗ Street. *Print, Library of Congress Prints and Photographs Division, Detroit Publishing Company.*

the tower's design is the way it breaks with the city's traditional rectangular street grid with its sloped front entrance at a southwest angle and set back in a large, triangular, stepped plaza. Its large columns rise in the entrance, breaking through the slanted windows and dramatically emphasizing the interior and exterior of the space. The building's Park Avenue sidewalk has large bronze plaques of some city landmarks, such as Lever House, which also breaks with the city's traditional street plan grid. The Architects Building, where the famous architectural firm of McKim, Mead & White had its offices, was located on this site in 1912.

On the southwest corner of East 40th Street, **90 Park Avenue** was the site of the Princeton Club from 1922 to 1960. F. Scott Fitzgerald frequented the club often when staying in the city. Fitzgerald used the club in his novel *This Side of Paradise*—his character Amory Blain spent his afternoons at the Plaza Hotel, followed by theater and dinner at the Princeton Club, just as did Fitzgerald on many occasions.

We now walk south on the east side of Park Avenue back past the block between East 40th Street and East 39th Street. We are passing the site of Andrew Haswell Green's (1820–1903) home at **99 Park Avenue**. Here on November 13, 1903, on the sidewalk in front of his home, Green was shot and killed by a deranged stranger in a case of mistaken identity. Green was a lawyer, New York City planner and civic leader who participated in or led such projects in Manhattan as Riverside Drive, Morningside Park, Fort Washington Park and Central Park. He was the head of the Central Park Commission (CPC) and was largely responsible for the CPC's choosing Olmsted and Vaux's plan for Central Park despite resistance from Tammany Hall politicians. In 1897, Andrew H. Green chaired the committee that drew up the plan of amalgamation consolidating the five boroughs into New York City—before 1898, Manhattan was New York City.

Now, on the same block but on the west side of Park Avenue there stood a modern, two-story, Georgian-styled, eight-room, all-steel "House of the Modern Age" from June to November 1936. It was designed by William Van Alen for Better Homes in America (an industrial organization). CBS broadcast three radio programs per week from the house, and more than 166,000 people paid ten cents to visit it. Mayor LaGuardia broke ground for the building, and Eleanor Roosevelt laid the hearthstone. The purpose of the cottage was to demonstrate what a dollar could buy in the construction field on one of the city's most expensive sites.

William Van Alen is the same architect who designed the Chrysler Building, located just three blocks from here. Ironically, this was one of the

Number 59 Park Avenue, Church of Our Savior.

few commissions he got after designing one of the city's iconic Art Deco skyscrapers. Van Alen was severely criticized for getting a mechanic's lien on the Chrysler Building in order to obtain his million-dollar commission. He never did get another commission for a skyscraper.

Walking down Park Avenue to the southeast corner of East 38th Street, at **59 Park Avenue**, is the Church of Our Savior, a Roman Catholic church that opened in 1959 and was designed in a Neo-Romanesque style by architect Paul W. Reilly that gives the church the appearance of being much older. The interior has a Neo-Baroque ceiling and a tabernacle crafted in the studios of Arte Granda in Madrid, Spain, in a Renaissance style and is surmounted by a dome that represents the vault of heaven.

Aside from the fact that because of the small building area, the rectory was built on the roof just south of the bell tower, the design of the church is historically correct, except for the other inconsistency of having the air-conditioning mechanism located in the bell tower, displacing the carillon (a set of stationary bells in the church tower that can be played by hand or by a pedal action). The inconsistencies are not really noticeable from the street, but the carved *Gallery of Kings* above the front entrance is quite noticeable.

Adjacent to the church, at **57 Park Avenue**, is a nice example of a French urban townhouse in the Beaux Arts, French Renaissance style of Louis XVI. The façade's first floor is heavily rusticated and has an impressive cornice that is supported by heavy, paired, guttae-adorned modillions that are linked by swags and serves as a balcony setting off the main portion of the façade. The second and third stories are pierced by segmental arched openings with bracketed keystones. The second story has French doors with carved stone relief panels above the transoms depicting classically inspired figures of children singing and playing musical instruments. The third floor has casement windows with ornate wrought-iron railings; the windows are flanked by ornate incense burners, swags and bucranium carved in relief on top of pilasters. The fourth floor rises over a modillion cornice and a grooved frieze decorated with bell flowers. The fifth floor (roof) has a dentil cornice and a parapet that sets off the slate-covered mansard roof and copper-clad dormers. The sixth floor, not wholly visible from the street, has a wrought-iron railing and a parapet that are visible.

This mansion was designed by Horace Trumbauer and built between 1909 and 1911 for Adelaide L. Townsend Douglas (1852–1935) about a year after she divorced William P. Douglas (1842–1919), who developed Douglaston on Long Island. Douglas was vice-commodore of the New York Yacht Club. He owned the schooner *Sappho* and successfully defended

Adelaide L. Townsend Douglas. *Ink drawing by Sharon Florin.*

the America's Cup in 1871 against Britain's *Livonia*. Adelaide L. Townsend Douglas was a socialite and the well-known "secret" mistress of J.P. Morgan, who was frequently seen entering the mansion by its backyard entrance.

The mansion is now home to the Guatemalan Permanent Mission to the United Nations and is also both a New York City landmark and a national landmark. The lot is twenty-five feet wide, and the mansion is six stories, plus a basement. Its interior has been remodeled extensively over the years, but the façade remains intact.

Now we will reenter the Murray Hill Historic District and go to **103 East 37ᵗʰ Street**, which was built between 1909 and 1911 as the Augusta Bliss Reese Townhouse. In 1907, William W. Reese, a real estate broker and

Number 103 East 37th Street, former A. Bliss Reese Mansion.

Columbia University graduate, married Augusta in Grace Church. The wealthy couple summered abroad and began looking for a suitable residence that fall. They chose the Murray Hill neighborhood for their home because it was exclusive, but its old brownstones were out of fashion. In 1901, James Lanier and his wife, Harriet, replaced two old houses with a grand limestone residence in the latest Beaux Arts style at 123 East 35th Street. One year later, Thomas Benedict Clarke had Stanford White replace the brownstone façade of 22 East 35th Street with an updated Neo-Georgian design. The Reeses followed suit and commissioned architects Foster, Gade & Graham to design a five-story, Beaux Arts–styled townhouse that cost about $50,000 to build.

The rusticated limestone façade is pretty much as it was in 1911, with three parts, each separated by a shallow course of carved wave moldings ("doing the wave," see chapter 4). A broad set of three steps from the sidewalk lead to polished wooden double entrance doors. The tall French windows of the second and third floors open to small ornate cast-iron balconies. The fifth floor hides behind a stone balustrade over a bracketed cornice. On top is a mansard roof with three copper-framed dormers.

Augusta Bliss Reese was the treasurer of the Bellevue Hospital Tuberculosis Clinic and a member of the National Tuberculosis Association in 1915 (the same year that she inherited $25,000 from the estate of her sister, Catherine Anita Bliss, who had lived on Park Avenue). Mrs. Reese was fervently active in fundraising and charity events related to tuberculosis. William W. Bliss was active in his real estate business and as the senior warden at the Church of the Transfiguration on East 29th Street (the "Little Church Around the Corner").

In March 1942, the Reeses were traveling on the Taconic State Parkway in Millwood, New York, when they were involved in a tragic automobile accident. The seventy-nine-year-old William W. Reese was killed, and Augusta, then sixty-eight, was critically injured. Funeral services for Reese were held a few days later at his beloved "Little Church Around the Corner." The townhouse was converted and remodeled twice inside (the façade remains intact except for the garden on the roof). The townhouse now has an apartment on each floor.

Now we walk back to Park Avenue, leaving the historic district and crossing over to the center mall at East 37th Street, where there is a plaque that honors Mary Lindley Murray. The stone was placed here in her honor in 1903, and a plaque was installed in the stone in 1926 and replaced in 1994. Mayor Fiorello LaGuardia honored Mary Murray by christening a Staten Island steamboat the *Mary Murray* in 1938. There were two Broadway plays written and produced telling her story. *Dearest of Enemy* opened in 1925, was written by Robert Sherwood, and *Small War on Murray Hill* was written by Rogers and Hart, opening posthumously in 1955.

According to the Broadway plays, Mary Lindley Murray and her daughters engaged General William Howe and his staff in conversation and entertained them—joking about her "American friends" and the like—Mary gave the general cake, wine, a warm bath, steamed clams, lemon soufflé, pheasant and, finally, herself—realizing that every moment the general dallied gained precious time for Generals Washington and Putman to regroup their scattered forces. At that moment, there was no resistance, and had General Howe led his troops and established a line across Manhattan Island, he would have cut the Continental army in half, and it may not have been able to survive.

The Murrays had twelve children, of which five survived: three daughters (Mary, 1752–?; Beulah, 1762–1790; and Susannah, 1764–1808) and two sons (Robert Lindley, 1745–1826; and John, 1758–1819). Only Mary L. Murray and her daughters were at the farm when General Howe and his officers arrived. The earliest record of this story dates back to the journal of James Thacher, MD, a surgeon in the Continental army who wrote about the military events during the Revolutionary War. The entry in his journal that refers to this incident reads:

> *The British generals…repaired to the house of a Mr. Robert Murray, a Quaker and friend of our cause; Mrs. Murray treated them with cake and wine, and they were induced to tarry two hours or more, Governor Tryon frequently joking her about her American friends. By this happy incident general Putnam, by continuing his march escaped…It has since become almost a common saying among our officers, that Mrs. Murray saved this part of the American army.*

The part of the entry that refers to her husband, Robert, as "a friend to our cause" is known to be incorrect. Although Robert Murray may have put forth a superficial front feigning loyalty to the patriotic cause, his continued trading with England must have been known by Howe and was probably the reason he didn't question Mary Murray's motives for distracting him, along with the fact that the Murrays' son Robert Lindley (1745–1826), though estranged from his father, Robert, was also known as a English sympathizer. In fact, Robert Lindley Murray was exiled to England after the Revolution and became the largest-selling author in the world. Lindley Murray wrote eleven English textbooks that sold more than 15.5 million copies in the first forty years of the nineteenth century. The fact that his *English Reader*, an anthology, had an enormous, worldwide circulation supports the idea that the book must have influenced hundreds of thousands (maybe millions) of children in America and England in ways not immediately apparent. The book's contents included many civic humanistic ideas, based on the Enlightenment, that strongly supported the spread of antislavery sentiment. Because of the *English Reader*'s place in our nation's schools, our children were exposed, from colonial times into antebellum America, to the civic humanist and republican ideas of the seventeenth- and eighteenth-century Enlightenment.

One could make the point that by saving the Continental army from devastation, Mary Lindley Murray saved the colonies from English domination and made the United States of America possible. Moreover, her son Robert Lindley was a major contributor to the defeat of slavery in America. The *English Reader* sold more than 5 million books in the United States just before the Civil War. Abraham Lincoln called it "the best schoolbook ever put in the hands of an American youth." The two events are connected not only because Robert Lindley was Mary L. Murray's son but also because of the fact that if we lost the Revolutionary War, Robert Lindley Murray would not have been banished to England and may not have written the English textbooks.

It is likely that Mary L. Murray was somewhat on her own with her strong patriotic views—not only were her husband and sons English sympathizers, but it also became evident that her three daughters were also somewhat sympathetic to the English, given whom they chose to marry. Mary married Ichabod Barnet, who conspired with Robert Murray to continue trade with the English despite the Quaker boycott. Beulah married Martin Hoffman, a Loyalist, and Susannah married Gilbert Colden Willet, a physician and a member of the King's Loyal American Forces. At the time of General Howe's visit, Susannah was twelve years old, Beulah was fourteen years old and Mary was twenty-four years old, and their sympathies seemed to favor the English over the American revolutionaries. Mary Lindley Murray was able to manipulate her daughters so that they would not reveal her patriotic views, but moreover she enlisted their aid with the conversation, entertainment and dining that was needed to keep the general and his officers distracted for a few valuable hours.

Mary Lindley Murray died in 1780. With her story duly recorded, the story passed into legend, and in the telling of most legends, you usually get one side

Number 38 East 37th Street, Union League Club, Park Avenue.

of the story. There is also General Howe's side, and even if he didn't dispute any part of Mary's story, the general may well have added some particulars that may or may not be significantly relevant. Howe can be criticized for being overly cautious and failing to take advantage of an unforeseen opportunity (the collapse of the Continental army's resistance at the encounter near Kip's Bay), but it should be said that he had already established a secure beachhead on Manhattan and had accomplished everything called for in his orthodox battle plan for that day. The general could and probably did claim that regardless of the conscious congeniality extended to him at the Murray mansion, he would not have moved until the next day, when all his troops, cavalry and artillery had landed and regrouped.

Now we walk to the northeast corner of Park Avenue and East 37th Street, and at **38 East 37th Street**, we find the Union League Club, opened in 1930. The club was founded in 1863 by Republicans who left the Union Club because it failed to expel Confederate sympathizers. Its founding members included Frederick Law Olmsted, who wanted to recruit a new generation of young, wealthy men so that the club could teach them the obligations and duties of an elite upper class; George Templeton Strong, who also believed that the club needed well-to-do New Yorkers; Alexander

T. Stewart; William Aspinwall; Robert B. Minturn; Henry Adams Bellows; and Oliver W. Gibbs.

In 1863, a few months after the Draft Riots exploded in Manhattan, the Union Club decided to emphasize its determination and unity with the Union cause. The club recruited, trained and equipped a Colored Infantry regiment (20th Regiment U.S. Colored Infantry) on Rikers Island. In 1864, along with members of the Union League Club on East 17th Street, the regiment marched to Canal Street and over to the Hudson River piers, where the regiment embarked for duty in Louisiana. During World War I, the club sponsored the famous Harlem Hellfighters (369th Infantry), which was commanded by William Hayward, a member of the club. A list of well-known members over the decades includes Ulysses S. Grant (eighteenth president of the United States and commanding general of the U.S. Army), Herbert Hoover (thirty-first president), Chester A. Arthur (twenty-first president), Theodore Roosevelt (twenty-six president, New York governor and Rough Rider), William T. Sherman (Union Civil War general), William Cullen Bryant (poet and editor of the *New York Post*), Peter Cooper (philanthropist and inventor), J.P. Morgan (Wall Street financier), John D. Rockefeller (founder of Standard Oil) and Charles H. Parkhurst (social reformer and clergyman).

This is the Union League Club's fourth clubhouse in Manhattan and has sixty bedrooms for members and guests, a variety of meeting rooms for business and social functions, an extensive reference and lending library, a distinguished art collection, an art gallery with rotating exhibits and a fitness center with international squash courts.

The Union League Club's façade is a New York City landmark, along with part of its interior, which constitutes an architectural ensemble formed by the entrance foyer leading to a grand staircase. The club was designed by Henry W. Morris (of Morris and O'Connor) with a moderate red brick, symmetrical, Neo-Georgian façade that reflects motifs similar to earlier Park Avenue mansions, only on a grand ten-story scale. The 37th Street façade includes a curved double-height entrance pavilion and oversized Palladian-style windows, along with a large pediment framing a cartouche and the club's initials. The rectangular panels flanking the entrance are influenced by the Art Deco style. A second entrance on Park Avenue leads to dining facilities and a fourth-floor lounge originally intended for members' wives and daughters, and the entrance crowned by a lintel with four female faces. This relief also suggests the influence of the Art Deco style.

The *AIA Guide to New York City* describes the red brick clubhouse as an "effete neo-Georgian pile," while the New York City Landmarks Preservation Commission report on October 25, 2011, refers to the clubhouse as a "fine example of a neo-Classical style clubhouse." And for what its worth (not much, I expect), my personal opinion is that they are both partially correct and that the clubhouse is a fine example of a Neo-Georgian clubhouse.

As we walk up Park Avenue toward East 38th Street, we can look across Park Avenue and have a nice view of the Adelaide L.T. Douglas Mansion and the Church of Our Savior before we arrive in front of **56 Park Avenue**. The Scandinavia House is an office building, opened in 2000, that also houses the Nordic Center in America and the American Scandinavian Foundation. The building is an example of the Late Modern (International Style III) style and was designed by the Polshek Partnership of New York City.

The Scandinavia House showcases the cultures and traditions of five Nordic countries: Denmark, Finland, Iceland, Norway and Sweden. Its galleries features a variety of exhibitions, and it offers programs such as films, concerts, lectures and events that include the visual and performing arts, literature, technology, science and business. On view throughout the center are selections of important modern and contemporary paintings by well-known artists on long-term loan from national Nordic museums. The Shop at Scandinavia House offers objects of Scandinavian design, books and music for sale. Scandinavia House's AQ Café is a lovely spot for lunch or refreshments. Scandinavia House includes a 168-seat Victor Borge Hall for performances and lectures, the Heimbold Family Children's Learning Center (which offers regular programs and activities for children and families) and the Halldór Laxness Library.

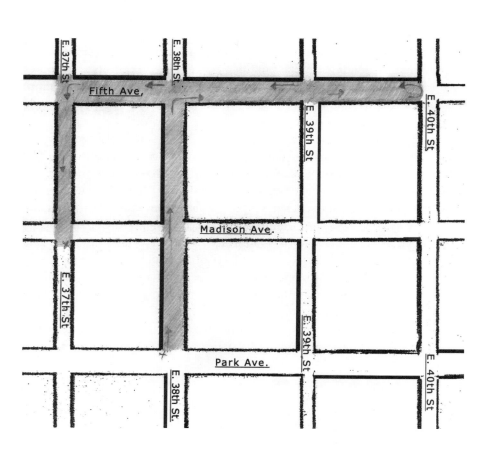

Chapter 6

MILLIONAIRES, SUFFRAGETTES AND HUMANITY'S HERO

East 38th Street, Madison Avenue, Fifth Avenue and East 37th Street

We will turn off Park Avenue and walk west on East 38th Street toward Madison Avenue. On the north side of this block is the site where William R. Grace (1831–1904) had his mansion before moving to the Upper East Side (31 East 79th Street). The Grace mansion (demolished) was adjacent to 31 East 38th Street. W.R. Grace was the first Irish-born Roman Catholic elected mayor of New York City in 1880, and he was reelected 1884. While mayor, he accepted the Statue of Liberty from France and donated the land for Grant's tomb.

Grace established the W.R. Grace and Company in 1866, and it still prospers today. In 1897, William R. Grace and his brother, Michael, established the Grace Institute at Tenth Avenue and West 60th Street for the purpose of educating immigrant women in domestic sciences and occupations that would make them self-supporting. The institution was dedicated to the memory of their parents.

In the 1960s, the Grace Institute moved to 1233 Second Avenue, where it is still providing tuition-free practical job training programs for women from diverse racial, ethnic and religious backgrounds who range in age from late teens to seniors (such as recent high school graduates, someone ready to change their career or someone ready to advance in their current position). Over the decades, the institute has changed along with the transforming needs of the city's workforce. It offers valuable, up-to-date office training along with computer, business skills and fashion merchandising training together with career advice and job-placement assistance. Since 1897, more than 100,000 women have graduated from Grace Institute. Walk to the corner of Madison Avenue

Numbers 36, 38 and 40 East 38th Street, former townhouses.

Theodore A. Havemeyer. *Ink drawing by Sharon Florin.*

At the southwest corner of **East 38ᵗʰ Street and Madison Avenue** was the site of 244 Madison Avenue, the Theodore A. Havemeyer mansion (demolished). The corner mansion was on much a larger lot, about twice the size of the mid-block mansions. It was facing Madison Avenue and had a French Second Empire Mansard roof; it was surrounded by a front lawn and a cast-iron fence (about seven feet tall) that extended around the sides of the house. The Havemeyer family mansion was built in 1868 and remodeled in 1892 by the society architect Richard Morris Hunt. It was just one of Murray Hill's many Gilded Age mansions owned by elite New Yorkers of the era.

Theodore Augustus Havemeyer (1839–1897) and his brother, Henry Osborne, inherited a sugar refinery from their father, William Havemeyer (1804–1874), an American businessman who was elected mayor of New York City in 1845 and 1846. By the 1890s, Theodore and Henry had made their own fortunes and controlled 98 percent of the sugar industry in the United States.

Theodore Havemeyer was also the Austrian consul general in New York City for twenty-five years, the first president of the U.S. Golf Association, the cofounder of the Newport Country Club and host to the first U.S. Open in 1895. But in some ways, fortune didn't shine on the Havemeyer family. In May 1897, Theodore Havemeyer's married son, Charles F., met an odd death. His wife, Camilla, heard a shot and found him in his room sitting in a chair with a bullet wound in his forehead and a navy revolver on the floor beside him. It was never determined if it was accidental or intentional. There was no apparent reason for suicide.

Less than three years later, in July 1900, Theodore Havemeyer's oldest married daughter, Mrs. Natalie Mayer, also met with a peculiar death, dying of a gunshot wound just under her heart (her mother, Mrs. Havemeyer, and a man named Clinton Page were present). Again it was never determined if the wound was accidental or intentional, as there were conflicting stories, and there was no apparent reason for suicide.

Number 260 Madison Avenue is a huge, white, brick, twenty-two-story office building that opened in 1953 and occupies the entire block between East 38ᵗʰ Street and 39ᵗʰ Street. We can walk on East 38ᵗʰ Street toward Fifth Avenue and stop in front of 15 East 38ᵗʰ Street. There is a small storefront (BK Shoe Repair) in the side of the office building. If we travel back in time to Murray Hill's Gilded Age, there would have been any number of interesting people living in Murray Hill, but the two sisters who lived here in a townhouse at **15 East 38ᵗʰ Street** were, by far, the most controversial and interesting the neighborhood had to offer.

From 1870 to 1877, the townhouse (demolished) was the home of Victoria Woodhull (1838–1927) and her family. Victoria's family included her sister, Tennessee Claflin; her second husband, Colonel James H. Blood; and her ex-husband (first), Dr. Canning Woodhull, MD, who was unable to work because of his addiction to alcohol and morphine. Victoria had her son, Byron (born with serious mental handicaps), and daughter, Zula Maud, with Canning Woodhull and divorced him after eleven years of marriage. A few years later, after Victoria married Colonel Blood, Canning showed up at her Murray Hill doorstep, destitute and sick. Victoria ended up supporting him (again) and allowed him to live in her Murray Hill townhouse with her family because the doctor was able to take care of their children and was especially qualified to care for their son with his mental deficiencies. The newspapers had a field day.

Victoria and her sister, Tennessee, made their first fortune as teenage spiritualists and their second fortune as Wall Street brokers. Victoria was a woman at least one hundred years ahead of her time. She ran for president of the United States in 1872, becoming one of the most famous women in the country. She campaigned for the eight-hour workday, graduated income tax, social welfare programs and profit sharing. She was a bundle of contradictions and offered her hospitality to prostitutes and royalty alike. Even though she was opposed to the organized Christian religion, Victoria lived by its principles: she fed the hungry, cared for the sick and visited prisoners. Victoria believed that living by the principles was more important than preaching. Victoria and Tennessee owned a newspaper that was the first to print an English version of Karl Marx's *Communist Manifesto* in America, and yet they were also the first women to own a brokerage house on Wall Street, where they made their second fortune. They were controversial, unique and courageous.

In 1870, with the assistance of the influential Cornelius Vanderbilt, Victoria and Tennessee became the first female stockbrokers to open a Wall Street brokerage firm, Woodhull, Claflin and Company, at 44 Broad Street. Some papers may have jokingly referred to the sisters as the "Bewitching Brokers" or the "Queens of Finance," and some of the men's journals made nasty insinuations about sex, but the fact is that they made a fortune on the New York Stock Exchange. The sisters had befriended Cornelius Vanderbilt, and he had a high regard for their skills as spiritualists and mediums. There was a strong rumor that he had asked Tennessee to marry him and she refused. When a reporter asked Tennessee about the rumor, she reportedly replied, "I would rather be a broker and a mistress than a wife and a chattel."

Victoria Woodhull speaking before the U.S. Congress, 1871. *Courtesy of the Library of Congress.*

Also in 1870, the sisters were the first women in the United States to found, publish and run a newspaper, *Woodhull and Claflin's Weekly*. Their paper advocated a single moral standard for men and women, equal rights in marriage, women's suffrage, short skirts, sex education, free love, spiritualism, vegetarianism, socialism and licensed prostitution. Victoria's second husband, Colonel James H. Blood, wrote many of the articles published in their paper.

In 1871, *Frank Leslie's Illustrated Newspaper* displayed an illustration (from a wood engraving) of Victoria Woodhull's speech in Washington, D.C., on January 11 in front of the Judiciary Committee of the U.S. House of Representatives in which she argued for the rights of women to vote on basis of the Fourteenth and Fifteenth Constitutional Amendments.

On November 20, 1971, in Steinway Hall at 73 East 14th Street, Victoria Woodhull made one of her public statements concerning a woman's right to be free to love as she choose: "Yes, I am a Free Lover. I have an inalienable, constitutional and natural right to love whom I may, to love as long or as short a period as I can; to change that love every day if I please, and with that right neither you nor any law you can frame have any right to interfere." The newspapers had a great time exploiting it.

On May 10, 1872, the Equal Rights Party held its convention at Apollo Hall on the east side of Broadway between Canal and Walker Streets in Manhattan and nominated Victoria Woodhull as its presidential candidate. The party also nominated Frederick Douglass as its candidate for vice president of the United States. Victoria Woodhull used her offices at 44 Broad Street as campaign headquarters when she ran for president of the United States. Needless to say, she lost the election; at that point in time, it was inevitable.

In October 1876, Victoria Woodhull and Colonel Blood divorced. Less than a year later, she left for England with her two children, her sister and her mother. In London, Victoria lectured on topics such as "The Human Body, the Temple of God." It was at one of these lectures that she met John Biddulph Martin, a wealthy banker. They fell in love and married on October 31, 1883, despite his family's disapproval. From 1892 to 1901, Victoria Woodhull Martin, with the help of her daughter, Zula Woodhull, published the magazine *The Humanitarian*. When her husband died in 1901, Victoria gave up publishing and retired, establishing her residence at her manor house in Bredon's Norton, Worcestershire, England. She died in 1927 the wealthy widow of a British banker.

You have to admit that the two sisters came a long way, especially when you consider the fact that they were born in the small rural frontier town of Homer, Ohio, into an impoverished family. Victoria was the seventh of ten children (six survived), and Tennessee was the youngest. Their father was Reuben "Buck" Claflin (a gristmill operator, con artist and snake oil salesman). Their mother was Roxanna (Roxy) Claflin, who was illiterate, quick-tempered, quick-witted and clairvoyant. When Victoria was eleven years old, the family was driven out of Homer by vigilantes because of her father's involvement with arson and fraud. She received very little formal education and spent most of her childhood with her family's traveling medicine show. Victoria was fourteen years old when she met (and fifteen when she married) Dr. Canning Woodhull, a drug-addicted alcoholic. At that point in time, her future seemed less than promising.

When we reach Fifth Avenue and East 38th Street, we might like to take a slight detour, turn right and walk to **455 Fifth Avenue**, the Mid-Manhattan Library at the southeast corner of East 40th Street. It was established in 1970 and houses the largest circulating collections of the New York Public Library. The Mid-Manhattan Library is five floors full of books (plus one floor is a computer lab and offers free Wi-Fi to anyone with a laptop, iPad or tablet).

Number 424 Fifth Avenue, Lord & Taylor.

This library offers programs for anyone interested in just about anything. I like to think of this library as a workingman's library because it caters to local office workers and students. It is a tremendous resource, and it has just about any book you might like. But do not confuse it with the main branch of the New York Public Library, located across Fifth Avenue between West 40th and West 42nd Streets, which is one of America's largest research libraries (you can not take the books out) and just falls outside Murray Hill. By 2018, the Mid-Manhattan Library plans to close at 455 Fifth Avenue and move across Fifth Avenue into the main branch—it will be a circulating library inside of the research library. When this happens, it will no longer be in the Murray Hill neighborhood.

We now can walk back down Fifth Avenue, passing Lord & Taylor Department Store between West 39th Street and West 38th Street at **424–434 Fifth Avenue**. It was founded as a dry goods store in 1826 on Catherine Street and has had several locations as it continued to move uptown before it opened here in 1914. If we stay on the east side of Fifth Avenue, we can appreciate the gray brick and limestone Neo-Renaissance façade's distinctive features, which include a prominent chamfered corner on West 38th Street and a deep, projecting copper cornice along Fifth Avenue, all designed by the well-known architectural firm of Starrett & Van Vleck. The store is well known for its annual Christmas window displays—a New York tradition that started more than eighty years ago. Also, Dorothy Shaver was Lord & Taylor's president from 1945 to 1959, the first woman to occupy such a position. This Lord & Taylor building is a New York City landmark.

It is a short walk along Fifth Avenue to the northwest corner of West 37th Street. This corner was the site of the Brick Presbyterian Church from 1857 to 1938 (demolished). The funeral of Mark Twain (Samuel Clemens) was held here on August 23, 1910. Twain (1835–1910) was a famous American author and humorist. Two of his best-known works were *The Adventures of Tom Sawyer* (1876) and *Adventures of Huckleberry Finn* (1885), the latter of which is sometimes referred to as "the Great American Novel." He died in his country home in Redding, Connecticut, and is buried at Woodlawn Cemetery in New York City.

On the southwest corner of 37th Street and Fifth Avenue is **402–404 Fifth Avenue**, the Stewart & Company Building, a New York City landmark building built in 1914 by Robert Goelet (from one of the wealthiest families of the Gilded Age and Whitney Warren's nephew). Goelet commissioned the architectural firm of Warren & Wetmore, which designed this loft building in one of its most unusual styles—one that reflects the diverse influences of the eighteenth-century British Neoclassical movement (the delicate blue and white terra-cotta ornaments are reminiscent of John Wedgwood's colored stoneware). It also reflects the style of the late nineteenth-century Chicago Skyscraper School of Architecture (a steel-frame building with masonry cladding, terra-cotta designs, large areas of glazing and a tripartite vertical design that can symbolize the metal frame of the building). Two important proponents of the eighteenth-century British Neoclassical movement were John Wedgwood and Robert Adam. Louis Sullivan was the most important proponent of the Chicago School. Warren & Wetmore gave us Grand Central Terminal and a number of other architectural gems.

Located on the southeast corner of 37th Street and Fifth Avenue is **397–409 Fifth Avenue**. It was built as the Tiffany & Company Building and was opened in 1906. The building is a New York City and a national landmark building, designed by McKim, Mead & White in a Venetian Renaissance style modeled after the majestic sixteenth-century Palazzo Grimani in Venice (this seems appropriate since Grimani was once Venice's wealthiest family, and Tiffany is America's most prestigious jewelry store). The white marble façade gives the impression of a three-story building—actually, it is seven stories tall. It is a sophisticated commercial design, with large plate glass

Number 233 Madison Avenue, De Lamar Mansion entrance.

windows, Corinthian piers and columns and an imposing entablature on top. Tiffany, America's foremost purveyor of jewelry and luxury items, moved up to East 57th Street and Fifth Avenue in 1940. Tiffany had earlier stores on Union Square and on Broadway between Prince and Spring Streets.

We will now walk east on East 37th Street. As we approach the northwest corner of Madison Avenue, we will see the ornate entrance of 232 Madison Avenue on East 37th Street. This Neo-Gothic office building designed by Polhemus & Coffin opened in 1925. We will walk to the northeast corner of East 37th Street and Madison Avenue to see quite a surprise at **233 Madison Avenue**—an overachiever, a mansion that really looks like a mansion. This building was built as the Joseph Raphael De Lamar House between 1902 and 1905, designed by C.P.H. Gilbert in a robust Beaux Art style with a towering mansard roof decorated with copper cresting and shell motifs. The main façade on East 37th Street is divided horizontally and vertically in tripartite divisions. Its entrance is deeply recessed, with double oak doors and a stone balcony on top and an elliptical arched window. The mansion is one of the most spectacular in the city. On one side of the mansion, there is a large, modern metal plate that is flush with the sidewalk and covers an iron grate with glass inserts. It is the top of an elevator that used to take the De

Jan Karski's seated statue.

Lamar limousine down to the basement; in fact, the elevator still functions. The Joseph Raphael De Lamar House is Murray Hill's largest mansion. It is a New York City and a national landmark building.

Joseph Raphael De Lamar (1843–1918) was a Dutch-born merchant seaman who made a fortune in mining and metallurgy during the California and Colorado Gold Rushes. De Lamar married Nellie V. Sands in 1893, they divorced in 1910 and he died in 1918 at the age of seventy-five, leaving an estate of $29 million. His obituary in the *Boston Daily Globe* described him as a "man of mystery" and an accomplished organist. Joseph De Lamar's only child was his daughter, Alice De Lamar (1901–1981). She never liked the mansion and left it a short time after his death, moving into a Park Avenue apartment instead. Alice is said to have inherited about $10 million; the Pennbrook estate on Glen Cove, Long Island; and the mansion in Manhattan. But unlike other heiresses of that era who flagrantly collected husbands, titles and misfortune, Alice De Lamar was a secretive heiress who seemed shy when not with her small group of friends. For a short time after leaving the mansion, she worked as a volunteer driver and mechanic for the Red Cross and became an advocate for better housing for workingwomen. Alice preferred to stay in the background, but nevertheless, she was an active benefactor and patron who supported artists, writers, choreographers and architects. She kept homes in Palm Beach, New York, Weston and Paris.

In 1923, the National Democratic Club purchased the mansion for its headquarters, and in 1973, the Republic of Poland bought the mansion for $900,000 to house its consulate general in New York. Sitting on a bench on the right side of the building's entrance is a seated statue of Jan Karski (1914–2000), a hero of the Polish underground/resistance during World War II. In 1942 and 1943, Karski reported to the Polish government in exile and to the Western Allies (the United States and Britain) about the destruction of the Warsaw Ghetto and the Nazi extermination camps in German-occupied Poland. Karski came to the United States and became a naturalized citizen in 1954. He studied at Georgetown University and earned a PhD. Karski also taught at Georgetown University. For forty years, he taught in the areas of east European affairs, comparative government and international affairs, becoming one of the most celebrated and notable members of Georgetown's faculty. In 1985, he published the academic study *The Great Powers and Poland*.

In 1995, Karski was interviewed by Hannah Rosen and gave his opinion about the failure of the Allies to rescue most of the Jews from mass murder by the German Nazis:

> *It was easy for the Nazis to kill Jews, because they did it. The allies considered it impossible and too costly to rescue the Jews, because they didn't do it. The Jews were abandoned by all governments, church hierarchies and societies, but thousands of Jews survived because thousands of individuals in Poland, France, Belgium, Denmark, Holland helped to save Jews. Now, every government and church says, "We tried to help the Jews," because they are ashamed; they want to keep their reputations. They didn't help, because six million Jews perished, but those in the government, in the churches—they survived. No one did enough.*

The seated statue was created by Karol Badyna, a sculptor from Poland who teaches at the Art Academy in Krakow.

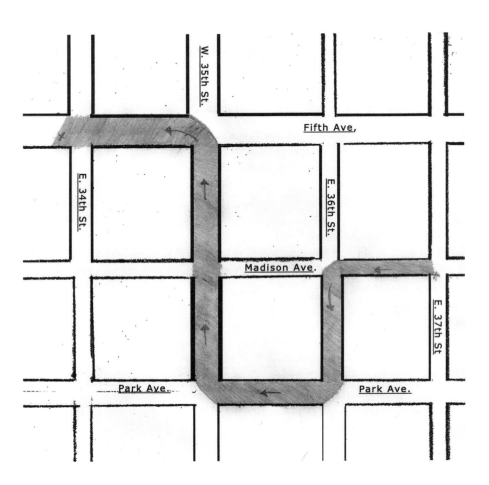

Chapter 7

J.P. Morgan Jr. Mansion to Alexander T. Stewart

East 37ᵗʰ Street, Madison Avenue, Fifth Avenue and East 34ᵗʰ Street

If we look at the southeast corner of East 37ᵗʰ Street and Madison Avenue, we will see **231 Madison Avenue**, built in 1852 as the Phelps Stokes Mansion. It is one of the few surviving freestanding brownstone mansions in Manhattan, and it was one of three brownstone Italianate-style Phelps family mansions built next to one another along Madison Avenue between East 37ᵗʰ Street and East 36ᵗʰ Street. J.P. Morgan bought the mansion for his son, J.P. Morgan Jr., who lived here from 1904 until 1944, when it was converted to the headquarters of the Lutheran Church in America. The building was acquired by the J.P. Morgan Library in 1988 and designated a New York City landmark in 2002.

J.P. "Jack" Morgan Jr. (1867–1943) was a financier and a philanthropist who inherited a major portion of his father's fortune. He was signatory to the establishment of the Federal Reserve in 1913 and loaned huge sums to France and Russia. All munitions purchased by Britain in the United States during World War I went through one of his firms. J.P. Morgan Jr. organized a syndicate of 2,200 banks and floated a loan of $500 million to the Allies. On July 4, 1915, "Frank Holt" (Eric Muenter) shot Morgan twice in the groin at his Glen Cove, Long Island home—the night before, Holt had set a bomb off at the U.S. Capitol protesting the United States' supplying armaments to Germany's enemies. In 1924, J.P. Morgan Jr. created the Pierpont Morgan Library as a public institution in memory of his father.

We will walk a short block to the northeast corner of Madison Avenue and East 36ᵗʰ Street. In 1880, J.P. Morgan Sr. (1837–1913) purchased the mansion that occupied this site, **225 Madison Avenue**, from John Jay

Left to right: The De Lamar Mansion, the Morgan Jr. Mansion and the Morgan Library Book Store/Museum.

Number 231 Madison Avenue, home of Mrs. J.P. Morgan in 1913, New York City. *Courtesy of Library of Congress Prints & Photographs Division, George Grantham Bain Collection.*

Phelps, who built the Italianate-style brownstone mansion in 1853. Morgan lived here from 1880 until he died in 1913, and by 1928, his son, J.P. Morgan Jr., had replaced the mansion with the Pierpont Morgan Library Annex. The architect for the annex was Benjamin W. Morris, who designed it in a Florentine Renaissance style in simple harmony and subordination to the Morgan library next door at 33 East 36th Street.

The annex holds the entire collection of J.P. Morgan's private library from the first floor of his old, demolished mansion and includes fifteenth- to nineteenth-century drawings, rare prints, manuscripts and more. Morgan collected the rarest and most expensive items—if you visit the library/museum, you will be impressed. The Pierpont Morgan Library Annex is a New York City landmark.

At the turn of the last century, during the Gilded Age, the name J.P. Morgan Sr. was world famous, and his range of power and influence was unmatched. There were and are many stories about his exploits, both private and public—such as those on his black, 241-foot yacht, the *Corsair*, as well as right here in his mansion. We know that he stopped the financial panic of 1907 in its tracks, but how did he do it? Provided leadership? Yes, but how? Actually, it was here in the library of his Murray Hill mansion that he saved the economy of the United States of America (and maybe of the world). There was a worldwide credit shortage. The situation was grim, with bank runs in Egypt, plunging Japanese stocks, a massive earthquake in San Francisco and the falling American markets, which lost a quarter of their value in the first nine months of 1907. Trust companies (hedge funds) failed, the stock market nearly closed because of a lack of funds and a number of large brokerage firms were in imminent danger of collapsing from too much leveraged debt—some things never seem to change.

When the panic hit in 1907, J.P. Morgan was in semiretirement, reporting to work periodically for one or two hours. But he reacted quickly. On Saturday, November 2, 1907, Morgan had a meeting with the heads of all of the city's solvent banks and trusts in the library of his Murray Hill mansion. The purpose was to hammer out a plan and an agreement whereby each entity contributed to a fund that totaled $25 million, and J.P. Morgan implemented the plan to bail out certain troubled banks with the funds and restore credibility, thereby stopping the panic. In theory, they agreed what should be done, but questions arose about how much each bank or trust would contribute and which institutions would be saved. While they were arguing, he had the doors locked and told them that they would not be allowed to leave until an agreement was reached. It took all night and into the next day, but they succeeded.

J.P. Morgan was acting as America's central bank, saving several trust companies and banks along with a leading brokerage house. Morgan rescued the New York Stock Exchange and New York City—both were facing bankruptcy. Earlier in his career, Morgan effected a solution to the gold crisis of 1895, financed U.S. Steel Corporation in 1901, arranged for the purchase of the Panama Canal Zone and financed General Electric—just a short list of a few of his major financial accomplishments. In 1880, J.P. Morgan's mansion on this site was the first private residence to be fully lit by electricity.

Before we leave J.P. Morgan, let's take a quick look at his softer side (yes, he had one, I think). The love of his life was Amelia (Memie) Sturges (1835–1862). She was the daughter of Jonathan Sturges, a well-known merchant and patron of the arts. When Amelia and her parents decided to take a European grand tour in 1859, Pierpont drew them an itinerary. He met them in London and saw Amelia every day for the last two weeks of their visit abroad, and he then escorted the family back across the Atlantic. In the spring of 1860, they made plans to marry, but she came down with a bad cough that didn't go away. They refused to postpone the wedding and were married on October 7, 1861. The couple went to the Mediterranean for a honeymoon cure. Another lung specialist in Paris confirmed the diagnosis of Amelia's illness as tuberculosis. Amelia wrote to her mother, "I wish you could see his loving devoted care of me, he spares nothing for my comfort & improvement." Despite his care, just four months after their wedding, Memie died in February 1862. Pierpont was twenty-four years old, and even though he was told that she was fatally ill before the marriage, he was stricken with grief and fell into an emotional and mental collapse that lasted about a year. It may well be that he never really completely recovered emotionally from the tragic experience.

In 1865, Morgan married his second wife, Frances Tracey, and had four children by her (three daughters and a son).

Next to the Morgan Library Annex is the Morgan Library at **33 East 36ᵗʰ Street**. It was built by J.P. Morgan in 1906 to house his private collection, including works by Cranach the Elder, Hans Memling, Cima da Conegliano (Giovanni Battista Cima) and other European artists. Also included were manuscripts by major literary and historical figures, such as Charles Dickens's *A Christmas Carol*, Henry David Thoreau's *Journals* and Thomas Jefferson's letters to his daughters, as well as important materials

Number 33 East 36th Street, Morgan Library.

from Jane Austin, Charlotte Brontë, Lord Byron, Albert Einstein, John Keats, Abraham Lincoln, John Milton, John Steinbeck, Voltaire and more.

The library's exterior and interior is a New York City landmark and its exterior is also a national landmark. The library was designed by Charles Follen McKim of McKim, Mead & White and is considered by many to be his masterpiece. Its design integrates sculpture, painting and architecture symbolizing the turn of the last century's ideal of "unity of design."

The library is styled after a classical Italian Renaissance villa, with its main entrance forming the design of a Palladian window, flanked by four paired Ionic columns backed by a deep porch that is decorated with a groin vaulted ceiling, pilasters and arches. Also, there are sculptured panels by Adolph Weinman: *Truth with Literature*, *Philosophy*, *History*, *Oratory*, *Astronomy* and *Music Inspiring the Arts*.

In front of the library, there stands a pair of lionesses by sculptor Edward Potter—he later did their mates for the New York Public Research Library. I can't help but speculate that the reason Potter chose male lions to be symbolic protectors of our heritage and culture in front of the public library is because the male lion is the king of the beasts and is known as the protector of his lair (the cubs and the female) from all outside danger. And maybe Potter chose female lionesses in front of the Morgan Library as symbols of predators, since the lioness is the predator, the one that does the hunting and brings home the kill for the lion and cubs to eat—the cultural treasures within were acquired by the private wealth of a kind of financial predator.

Let's walk on East 36th Street to Park Avenue, make a right turn and walk on Park Avenue to the corner of East 35th Street. On the northeast corner of East 35th Street and Park Avenue is **23 Park Avenue**, the James Hampden Robb and Cornelia Van Rensselaer Robb Mansion. It is a five-story mansion built between 1888 and 1892. The house was acquired by the Advertising Club in 1923 and converted into apartments (co-ops) in 1977. The former mansion is one of many New York City landmarks designed by Stanford White of McKim, Mead & White and is considered one of Stanford White's best Italianate-style urban residential designs. Its classically designed five-story façade incorporates a wealth of Renaissance-inspired details, presented in iron spot Roman brick with brownstone and terra-cotta trim over a high brownstone base. There is a pillared brownstone balcony over the entrance and a delicately crafted cast-iron balcony. The second floor has an oriel window on its south façade.

James Hampden Robb (1845–1911) was a former cotton broker, banker, New York assemblyman, New York state senator and president of the Union Club. Robb was intensely involved with the Democratic Party. While the mansion was being built, he was also serving as the New York City parks commissioner from 1887 to 1890. James and Cornelia Robb filled their mansion with rare art, antiques, sixteenth-century Persian rugs and Gobelin tapestries along with paintings by Rubens, Van Dyck and Emmanuel. In 1911, James Robb died in the mansion. Cornelia Robb lived in the mansion for a year. Then, in April 1912, she sold most of the furnishings at a much-publicized auction at the Plaza Hotel. The *New York Times* reported that the Metropolitan Museum of Art purchased a sixteenth-century terra-cotta *Madonna and Child* and other items, including a seven- by twelve-foot Persian carpet that sold for $22,000.

By this point, Park Avenue had changed. One by one, the grand mansions were falling, replaced by office buildings. Cornelia Robb leased her Italianate mansion as a boardinghouse and moved northward. It wasn't long before it was purchased by the Advertising Club.

If we walk on East 35th Street toward Madison Avenue and stop in front of **22 East 35th Street**, we can see a house (probably Italianate in style) that was built on this site in about 1867 for the Howland family. The house was reconstructed and redesigned as the Thomas and Fanny Clark House

Number 23 Park Avenue, J.H. Robb Mansion.

between 1901 and 1902 by Stanford White in a Colonial or Georgian Revival style with red and gray Flemish bond brickwork and an unusual, graceful, medieval-inspired, multi-paned, two-story bowed window (inspired by the British architect Richard N. Shaw's work in the 1870s and '80s) that is the prominent feature of the façade. It has contrasting stone and metal details and a rusticated ground floor with a classically inspired entrance portico. It all came together in 1902 as an outstanding residential design in Murray Hill. After the reconstruction, the taxes on the house rose from $8,000 to $12,000 per year because of its increased value.

Thomas and Fanny Clark were friends of Stanford White, and Thomas was a well-known turn-of-the-century art collector, art dealer and decorator. His house here served as showcase for his varied collection, considered one of the finest collections of American art in the world. Ironically, the house was sold to the Collector's Club in 1937. The club was founded in 1896 and is dedicated to philatelic literature related to postal or fiscal history and to the collection and study of stamps, revenue stamps and stamped envelopes.

We are now walking on East 35th Street to the northeast corner of Madison Avenue. At **205–209 Madison Avenue** is the Episcopal Church

Number 22 East 35th Street, Collectors Club (Clark Mansion).

Church of the Incarnation and Parish House.

of the Incarnation and parish house, designed by Emel T. Litell in 1864 in a style described as thirteenth-century Decorative Gothic. The design's most prominent feature is its tall, broached, asymmetrically placed spire. The church was built of masonry and brownstone, with light-colored sandstone trim, and it also features tracery and shallow buttresses. The church was altered and enlarged by D. & J. Jardine in 1882 after a fire. Both the church and parish house are New York City and national landmarks. The rectory, referred to as the "parish house" since 1934, is next to the church and was completed in 1869. In 1905–6, it was rebuilt and redesigned by Edward P. Casey in a Neo-Jacobean style.

Inside the church are some of the finest pieces of ecclesiastical artwork in America. There are stained-glass windows by John LaFarge (*Calling of Peter and Paul* and *God the Good Vintner*, south wall), Louis Comfort Tiffany (*The Pilgrim*, south side of chancel), Tiffany Glass Company (*Angel of Victory Over Death*, in the north wall) and Edward Burn-Jones and the William Morris Company. You will also find an oak communion rail with angels carved by Daniel Chester French, a reredos (altar) by Heins & LaFarge and a mural the *Adoration of the Magi* in the chancel (the space around the altar in the sanctuary), also by John LaFarge. The H.E. Montgomery Memorial, dedicated to the church's second rector, is the only work in New York City by H.H. Richardson.

In 1864, the church was erected as an uptown chapel for Trinity Church right at the time when Murray Hill was developing as a prestigious neighborhood of the Gilded Age. This was the church where many members of the Roosevelt family chose to worship—their family pews took up half the width of the church.

Directly across Madison Avenue from the Church of the Incarnation, James and Sara Roosevelt had their mansion at 200 Madison Avenue, on the northwest corner of Madison Avenue and East 35th Street. They were the parents of Franklin D. Roosevelt, who was living here with his family in 1905 when he proposed to and married Eleanor Roosevelt. They lived here for a short time before taking a European honeymoon and moving into their own home at 125 East 36th Street (see chapter 3). They lived there until 1908, when they moved into a large double mansion built by his mother, Sara, on East 65th Street that they shared with her.

The building at 200 Madison Avenue today is known as the Astor Estate Building (among other names), a Neoclassical skyscraper designed by the architectural firm Warren & Wetmore, which gave us Grand Central Terminal. It was built between 1923 and 1926. As we reach the corner of 35th Street

Numbers 374–380 Fifth Avenue, J. Coleman Drayton Mansion. *Ink drawing on paper by Sharon Florin.*

Fifth Avenue entrance to the B. Altman Department Store.

and Fifth Avenue, if we look northward across Fifth Avenue, we will see the site where the J. Coleman Drayton Mansion was located, at 374–380 Fifth Avenue. The mansion was a wedding present from William B. and Caroline Astor when Drayton married their daughter Charlotte in 1883.

The building that occupies the entire block between East 35th and East 36th Streets and Madison and Fifth Avenues opened in this wealthy Gilded Age neighborhood in 1906 as the B. Altman Department Store, **351–357 Fifth Avenue**. It was completed by 1913. The building was designed by Trowbridge and Livingston to blend as much as possible (given its size) into this affluent neighborhood by using an Italian Renaissance palazzo style that was adopted by many of the Fifth Avenue mansions. Also, the façade, made of French limestone, blended well with other Murray Hill mansions because it was a stone previously used only on residential buildings. The building limestone base has tall, arched, recessed window bays that are flanked by Corinthian pilasters. Powerful projecting portals emphasize the entrances on Fifth and Madison Avenues with elegantly fluted Corinthian columns.

Benjamin Altman (1840–1913) and his father started with a small nineteenth-century storefront on East 10th Street and Third Avenue. In 1874, the family store moved to West 18th Street and Sixth Avenue (Fashion Row), and when Altman moved up here to Fifth Avenue in 1906, the store was already known as the Palace of Trade and as a trendsetter for women's fashion.

Benjamin Altman was a solitary man, a keen entrepreneur and an art lover. Shortly before he died in 1913 (a bachelor, he never married), Altman gave his $15 million art collection to the Metropolitan Museum of Art. He is probably best remembered as a considerate employer who was well ahead of his time. His department store had its own trade school and medical clinic for its employees. Also, it was the first department store to install restrooms and a subsidized cafeteria for its employees. It was also the first department store to shorten its sixty-four-hour workweek for employees. It was said that Benjamin Altman lived in the department store.

B. Altman closed in the 1980s, and the building was vacant until 1996, when the exterior was restored and the interior reconfigured for use by the City University of New York for its Graduate Center on Fifth Avenue; by the New York Public Library as the Science, Industry and Business Library on Madison Avenue; and by Oxford University Press.

As we continue on this tour of Murray Hill, I believe what becomes more apparent is that what sets Murray Hill apart is not its history as a prestigious neighborhood but rather the fact that at different points in time over the last 250 years, Murray Hill has been home to such a large and varied group of different individuals who have had a profound influence on our country's political, financial and cultural development. We can start with the Quakers (Robert Lindley Murray and Mary Lindley Murray; see chapter 5) and go on to include the Roosevelts (see chapters 3 and 7), Victoria Woodhull (see chapter 6), J.P. Morgan and J.P. Morgan Jr. (see chapter 6), Charles Lanier (see chapter 3) and George S. Bowdoin (see chapter 4), not to mention such artists and writers as Dashiell Hammett, F. Scott Fitzgerald (see chapter 4) Malvina Hoffman (see chapter 2) and others. But the next two stops are going to focus on the wealthy and prestigious history of Murray Hill—unfortunately, the mansions are long gone, but we will visit the sites, and I'll give you a brief history of their pasts.

We walk to the northeast corner of Fifth Avenue and 34th Street, and I'd like to mention that when B. Altman was constructed, they were forced to build around the M. Knoedler Gallery. B. Altman literally towered over the gallery, which occupied a four-story building three bays wide (about twenty-five feet on Fifth Avenue, extending back about fifty feet on East 34th Street). The gallery moved to 556 Fifth Avenue in 1911, and Altman demolished the building and extended his store to the corner.

Now we just look at the northwest corner of West 34th Street and Fifth Avenue. On this corner in 1869, Alexander Turney Stewart demolished

Intersection of 34th Street and Fifth Avenue, view north in 1925. *Ink drawing by Sharon Florin.*

the country mansion of the "Sarsaparilla King," Samuel P. Townsend, and built his own huge, extravagant, marble, French Second Empire–style mansion facing West 34th Street. At that time, Stewart was considered second only to the Astors in wealth, but he never did gain acceptance into the higher circles of New York society. Was Stewart trying to give the impression of having more wealth than the Astors by building his lavish mansion across the street from two plainer and smaller Astor mansions? Was he looking for social recognition?

Alexander T. Stewart (1803–1876) came from Ireland in 1823 and opened a small dry goods store. He seemed to have a cash flow problem and had a "going out of business sale" that did quite well. He kept "going out of business" until he was a millionaire. Of course, that is an oversimplification—there were government contracts and large, successful investments in factories along the way. In 1849, he opened the prototype for the world's first department store, the Marble Palace. The building is a New York City landmark, and it is still standing at the northeast corner

The Alexander T. Stewart Mansion and two Astor mansions. *Ink drawing on paper by Sharon Florin.*

of Broadway and Chambers Street. In 1859, he opened the world's largest cast iron building and the largest department store on Fashion Row, the Alexander Turney Stewart Store at the corner of Broadway and East 9th Street. It was demolished in 1956. Stewart was known for being very frugal, a good businessman and, most of all, honest. When he gave his word, he kept it. When he died in 1876, Stewart left his wife, Cornelia, an estate worth more than $50 million. She lived in the mansion until she passed away in 1886. Shortly afterward, the mansion was converted into the Manhattan Club, and by 1912, it had been replaced by the Knickerbocker Trust Bank (Columbia Trust Company).

Now the story gets interesting. On November 7, 1878, Stewart's ashes were stolen from a crypt at St. Mark's in the Bowery Cemetery between East 9th and East 10th Streets on the west side of Second Avenue. The ghouls sent a note demanding $250,000 along with a circle drawn on the note that was the exact size as a circle that had been drawn and left in the crypt, along with some handles from the coffin, to verify that they truly had Stewart's remains. The note was signed Henry T. Romaine. Henry Hilton, Stewart's partner and the executor of the estate, bargained for a lower price. Negotiations broke off. It was two years later when a frail, seventy-nine-year-old Cornelia Stewart heard from the thieves again, and this time, she decided to negotiate with them herself. The ne'er-do-wells offered a discounted price of $100,000 for the remains. But Cornelia felt that they had no one else to do business with—who else would pay anything for the remains? You might say that she reasoned that they (the thieves) were "going out of business" and needed to offer a really steep discount. Cornelia made them a one-time offer of $20,000. They took it, returned the remains and were never heard from again.

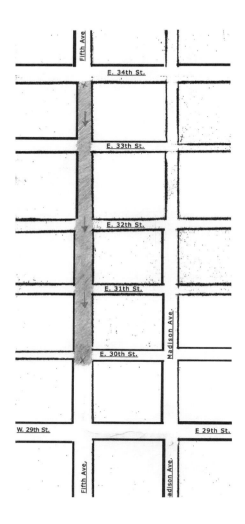

Chapter 8

THE ASTORS AND THE
EMPIRE STATE BUILDING TO THE
WILBRAHAM BUILDING

Fifth Avenue, West 34th Street, West 32nd Street and East 30th Street

Looking across the street at the southwest corner of 34th Street and Fifth Avenue, we can see the Empire State Building (see chapter 2). The history of the site itself (Fifth Avenue between 33rd Street and 34th Street), to a large degree, parallels the development of Murray Hill. It started with the John Thompson-Lawton farm on this site in the late eighteenth century. In 1827, William Backhouse Astor purchased the farmland as an investment, contemplating Manhattan's northward expansion; he could not have predicted the notoriety the site would yield or the stories that would be generated from this site. By the mid-nineteenth century, there was residential development, with two Gilded Age Astor mansions here. And at the turn of the twentieth century, there was commercial development of the site, with the Waldorf Astoria Hotel replacing the Astor mansions—both enjoying their heyday with legends revolving around family feuds, the 400 Elite, the Patriarch's Balls and the idiosyncrasies of wealthy New Yorkers. Then the Empire State Building replaced the hotel in 1931. Quite a history for a relatively small piece of real estate.

This was the site where Caroline Webster Schermerhorn Astor (1830–1908) and her husband, William Backhouse Astor Jr. (1830–1892), built their new mansion at 350 Fifth Avenue in 1859. They were soon surrounded by relations. Her brother-in-law, John Jacob Astor III, built an almost identical mansion for his son, William Waldorf Astor, at the northwest corner of 33rd Street and Fifth Avenue—the two mansions were separated by a garden. After the death of his wife, William Backhouse Astor Sr. (1792–1875) moved into a mansion on Fifth Avenue near 35th Street; two of his daughters were living at Madison Avenue and East 34th Street. Two of Caroline's married daughters were also living nearby: Charlotte, who married J. Coleman Drayton, was living at 374–380 Fifth Avenue, and another daughter was also on Fifth Avenue in Murray Hill. During the second half of the nineteenth century, the Astors tended to cluster together not so much because of familial affection but more because they lived on Astor properties for free.

Caroline W.S. Astor had four children (three girls and a boy). By the early 1870s, the girls were almost adults and ready for marriage. Caroline then decided to organize a proper New York society by holding a series of events, parties and balls, and those invited became the "accepted members" of society (the 400 Elite). At this point, her husband was not interested and was mostly absent (sailing on his Florida yacht), so Caroline enlisted S. Ward McAllister (sort of a super-snob of the day) to help her define who would be in the new society. They came up with a plan. Twenty-five New Yorkers (patriarchs) would give several balls each season, and each of the twenty-five would be responsible for inviting four ladies and five gentlemen. And "society" would be defined within this group. Over the years, the group of patriarchs grew to fifty. Caroline and Ward had the final say regarding who was in and who wasn't, and they had their own criteria and rules that needed to be adhered to—but not always.

When they increased the number of patriarchs from twenty-five to fifty, they (Caroline, Ward and the original patriarchs) allowed some new members that were considered "new money" but otherwise met the other criteria—the idea being that this group of new members would fight even harder to maintain the group's exclusivity. There were nuances, exceptions and complications, but generally speaking, the publicly acknowledged rules were as follows: anyone who made their money through retail trade was out (if you had three generations in New York, you had a chance); if you were flashy with your cash, you were out (if you had a box at the opera, maybe?); and there was also a daunting calling card etiquette, and if you didn't follow it, you were out. You also have to factor in that Caroline seemed to have a bias against Jews and Catholics, as there were no Jewish people on the list of the 400 Elite until she later changed her mind.

Here is one story that illustrates Caroline's (occasional) flexibility. Nellie (Ellin) Prince (1849–1941) was socially well connected, a prominent well-liked member of the 400 Elite and a very close friend of Caroline. Nellie was left penniless when her first husband, John A. Lowery, died in 1892. In order to support herself, Nellie opened and operated a tearoom in the

Knickerbocker Hotel. She became one of the earliest women in society to go into the retail trade. Caroline didn't hesitate to show her approval by bringing parties to the tearoom. Needless to say, Nellie's retail activities did not get her excluded from the balls or any part of the 400 Elite's activities.

Now we come to Alexander T. Stewart, an Irish immigrant who became one of the wealthiest men in America. He made his fortune in the retail trade. Stewart married well (Cornelia Clinch) and became a prominent citizen of the city. He was a member of the Union Club, the Century Association and the Union League, and newspapers noted his many charitable donations. Stewart even managed to be a pallbearer at the funeral of Margaret Armstrong Astor (Caroline's mother-in-law), and he lived directly across the street from Caroline. In the twenty-four years (1873–97) that Caroline Webster Schermerhorn Astor hosted her annual Patriarch's Ball in her mansion on the southwest corner of 34th Street and Fifth Avenue, she never invited Alexander T. Stewart or his wife, Cornelia—even though they lived across the street and were among the wealthiest families in America. Because Caroline chose to ignore them, they were denied access to *all* the parties, balls and events of the 400 Elite—she was drawing a line, making a point. But let's not to feel too sorry for the Stewarts, as they still were among the wealthiest families in the city and enjoyed an opulent lifestyle.

Now let's get back to Nellie operating her tearoom. It seems Nellie met and fell in love with James Speyer (1861–1941), a wealthy banker who happened to be Jewish. When James asked her to marry him, she was very much aware of the fact that Jewish people were not allowed entrance into the rarified society of the 400. Nellie went to Caroline and asked if she would be banned from society if she married Speyer. Caroline responded, "I don't think we have any alternative, for we are so fond of you. Marry him, my dear, if you want to. I for one will invite you both to my parties and I think everyone else will do the same."

After Nellie became Mrs. Ellin Prince Speyer in 1897, both her and husband were members of the 400 Elite. I'd say that Nellie was a bit ahead of her time in as much as she was the first woman in the 400 Elite to participate in the retail trade and was instrumental in gaining admission of one of the first Jewish persons into the 400 Elite; let's also not forget that she was twelve years younger than James Speyer, who built a mansion for Nellie on Millionaires' Mile in Manhattan.

Caroline Astor's reputation about the ultra-exclusivity of the 400 Elite was more legend than actual practice, as there seemed to be a certain amount of flexibility concerning which rules applied to which members—

you might call it favoritism, or you could say that Caroline thought more of her friendship with Nellie than she did of the silly rules.

In spite of, or maybe because of, her popularity, Caroline was having an ongoing feud with her nephew, William Waldorf Astor, who lived in the mansion at the corner of West 33rd Street and Fifth Avenue. In the early 1890s, William Waldorf Astor moved to England and replaced his mansion with the Waldorf Hotel (fourteen stories). It hovered over Caroline's mansion, causing her a great deal of anxiety—just as he hoped. She was trying to create an elite aristocracy, and to have this large commercial building overshadowing her mansion was frustrating to say the least. By 1895, Caroline had moved up to East 65th Street and Fifth Avenue on Millionaires' Mile and built a larger Astoria Hotel (eighteen stories) next to the Waldorf. Within two years, her son, John Jacob Astor IV, had negotiated a truce between Caroline and William Waldorf Astor.

Peacock Alley, with marble columns and mirrors on the walls and ceilings, was created as one of the main hallways to connect the two hotels, and the Waldorf Astoria came into being. It became a social center for the city, as well as a prestigious destination for visitors. Because of the tensions that existed between the two Astor families, Caroline had the architect Henry J. Hardenbergh (who designed both the Waldorf and the Astoria Hotels) provide a means to seal off the connecting corridors if the need arose.

The Astor family sold the Waldorf Astoria Hotel in 1918 to Coleman du Pont and Lucius M. Boomer. The hotel was later acquired by John Jacob Raskob, and by 1929, the original Waldorf Astoria had been demolished, as the Empire State Building was being built in its place. The new Waldorf Astoria Hotel opened in 1930 on Park Avenue between East 49th Street and East 50th Street.

Across from the Empire State Building at **336 Fifth Avenue**, at the northeast corner of East 33rd Street, is the A.T. Demarest & Company Building. It was built in 1890 and designed by Renwick, Aspinwall & Russell in a Renaissance Revival style, with iron spot bricks forming monumental four-story archways, providing much room for glass. The grand frieze is in high relief, with fancy brickwork and terra cotta under a large overhanging cornice.

The building was used for showrooms and offices for the carriages built by A.T. Demarest & Company, which was established in 1860, and by the 1880s, its New Haven factory had three hundred workers. From 1890 on, there was a transition period between the horse and carriage trade and the budding automobile industry. A.T. Demarest & Company moved to Broadway and West 57th Street in 1909 and started to sell Peerless

Number 336 Fifth Avenue, Demarest & Company Building.

automobiles. This building on East 33rd Street became a commercial office building. The *AIA Guide to New York City* has it listed as a New York City landmark. As we continue our walk down Fifth Avenue, I think it is a good time to mention that in 1937, when New York City extended Fifth Avenue north from 23rd Street to 42nd Street and sold surrounding land as building lots, it precipitated the development of Murray Hill as one of Manhattan's wealthiest neighborhoods. The development started immediately, with speculators building brownstone residences along Fifth Avenue. And going into the second half of the nineteenth century, the Murray Hill area quickly evolved to contain fashionable mansions of some of Manhattan's wealthiest families, along with a number of prominent churches. Ironically, within fifty years, the neighborhood would start to change again with the invasion of commercial development working its way up Fifth Avenue. The only thing that doesn't change in Manhattan is the fact that everything changes.

Now we walk down Fifth Avenue to the southwest corner of West 32nd Street to **316 Fifth Avenue**. The Kaskel & Kaskel Building opened 1903 as the headquarters and retail space for Kaskel & Kaskel Company, one of New York's leading haberdasheries, supplying shirts for the president of the United States and other wealthy men. The store was founded by Albert

Number 316 Fifth Avenue, Kaskel & Kaskel Building.

and Max Kaskel in 1867. This white marble Beaux Arts–style building was designed by architect Charles Berg. He created two three-story round arch openings, one facing Fifth Avenue and the other facing West 32nd Street; over each of the arches are cartouches with a carved K in the center. Over the fourth floor is a stone cornice with ornate brackets under a French

Mansard roof with great copper dormers on top. I'll never understand why this building isn't a New York City landmark—its architectural style sure seems to rate it.

As we continue down Fifth Avenue between East 32nd Street and East 31st Street, we pass **309 Fifth Avenue**. Going back in time, this address was the site of a small apartment building where Sinclair Lewis lived between 1917 and 1919 with his first wife, Grace. She was pregnant, and he started to write short stories, forty-four of them in two years. Before he moved here, Lewis was living at 69 Charles Street and was working reading manuscripts for a commercial publisher, making $12.50 per week. After leaving 309 Fifth Avenue, he wrote *Main Street*, the novel that made him famous, in 1920. Columbia University voted Sinclair Lewis the Pulitzer Prize in 1921, but its board of trustees refused to grant him the award—its members didn't agree with his version of small-town America. In 1925, Lewis was awarded the Pulitzer Prize by Columbia University for *Arrowsmith*, and he told them to keep it. In 1930, Sinclair Lewis was the first American to win a Nobel Prize for literature. And in the Nobel Committee's presentation speech, both *Main Street* and *Arrowsmith* were cited, and the prize was awarded to the author. You'd think maybe that the board of trustees in 1921 was a bit arrogant and made a big mistake—no one really cared or cares what its version of small-town America was. It should have awarded Lewis the prize (money) that the university's jury voted to award him. In 1998, the Modern Library ranked *Main Street* sixty-eighth on its list of the one hundred best English-language novels of the twentieth century.

A few blocks farther down on Fifth Avenue, we approach the northeast corner of East 30th Street at what used to be **291 Fifth Avenue** from 1905 to 1917 (the site that is now the Textile Building, 295 Fifth Avenue, since 1920). This was the site of 291 Gallery, also known as Little Galleries of the Photo-Secession, where Alfred Stieglitz (1864–1946) introduced a number of avant-garde European artists to America through his space located here, showcasing such new artists as Henri Matisse (1908), Henri Rousseau and Paul Cézanne (both 1910), Pablo Picasso (1911), Marcel Duchamp and many others. Stieglitz's contribution to our culture also includes the fact that his exhibitions here helped elevate recognition for art photography, making its status compatible with painting and sculpture. Alfred Stieglitz was born in Hoboken, New Jersey, his parents were German Jewish immigrants who nurtured his education, sending him to the Charlier Institute in Manhattan and then to study in Germany for several years. He returned to America in 1881. Stieglitz matured as an American photographer and as a modern art promoter was instrumental over his fifty-year career in making photography an accepted art form. He was married to painter Georgia O'Keeffe, whom many label as the "Mother of American Modernism."

Across Fifth Avenue at the northwest corner of West 30th Street, we will find **284 Fifth Avenue**, the Wilbraham Building. It was built between 1888 and 1890 as an apartment hotel featuring bachelor flats; each flat had a bedroom, a parlor and a bathroom but no kitchen. There was a communal dining room on the eighth floor. The building was designed with exceptionally fine detail (especially on the West 30th Street entrance) in a sophisticated commercial interpretation of Romanesque Revival style by the architectural firm D. & J. Jardine (David and John). It is a building that graces the corner with its rock-faced stonework, rounded arched openings, red Philadelphia brick and warm Belleville brownstone, all intermingled with a bit of cast iron on its façades.

The New York City Landmark Preservation Commission report of June 8, 2004, refers to the building's architectural style as being influenced by the Romanesque Revival style and making use of classical references, but the *AIA Guide to New York City* refers to the building's style as "Belle Époque crowned with a verdigris copper roof." Anyway you would like to describe the building, it is an impressive, historically styled building that mixes Romanesque Revival ornament with classical references, and it is no surprise that the building is a New York City landmark.

The building's interior was remodeled to include kitchens by 1935, probably a result of the increased popularity of gas cooking.

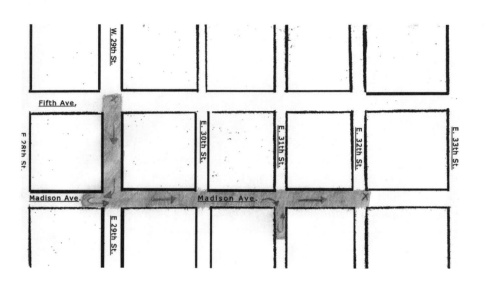

Chapter 9

THE MARBLE COLLEGIATE CHURCH TO ANDY WARHOL

Fifth Avenue, East 29ᵗʰ Street, Madison Avenue, East 31ˢᵗ Street, East 32ⁿᵈ Street, Park Avenue and East 33ʳᵈ Street

L et's walk a block farther down Fifth Avenue to the northwest corner of West 29ᵗʰ Street, **275 Fifth Avenue**. The Marble Collegiate Church was completed in 1854 and is so named because it was built out of solid blocks of marble quarried at Hastings-on-Hudson. It was designed by architect Samuel Warren with a complex mix of Gothic, Romanesque and classical forms, including fifteenth- or sixteenth-century Gothic Revival–style spires and delicately carved finials facing Fifth Avenue. Along West 29ᵗʰ Street, you have five thirteenth- or fourteenth-century Romanesque-inspired rounded arched windows and large buttresses that support the building's massive plans. The details are inspired by European architecture, but the overall impression is that of an American New England church, with its impressive central tower, a belfry, a clock, a spire and a weather vane. Octagonal turrets with pinnacles capped with molded cornices and carved finials complete the church.

The church had a major exterior restoration in the 1990s by Hall Partnership. The restoration included the installation of its first new stained-glass windows in nearly a century. The new windows, by Lamb Studios, reflect the church's image as an inclusive community by depicting the Pentecost with three children: one Asian, one black and one white. The earlier window that was replaced was by Frederick Wilson of Tiffany & Company in 1900 and 1911. The church is a New York City and a national landmark.

Marble Collegiate Church is one of four bodies under a single consistory that governs the Collegiate Reformed Protestant Dutch Church of the City of New York. The consistory is made up of elders, deacons and ministers.

Left: Number 275 Fifth Avenue, Marble Collegiate Church.

Below: Statue of Norman Vincent Peale.

The church was founded by the Dutch in New Amsterdam in 1628 and is the oldest Protestant congregation in America, with a continuous ministry since it began. The congregation's earliest organized services were held on what is now South William Street in the loft over a gristmill. In 1633, the congregation built its first church building on what is now 33 Pearl Street. The Marble Collegiate Church was built in 1854 when 23rd Street was the city limit and Fifth Avenue was a dirt road. The purpose of the cast-iron fence around the church's property was to keep cattle out of the churchyard. Today, the churchyard has two sculptures. A bronze life-size statue of Norman Vincent Peale, dedicated in 1998, was created by sculptor John M. Soderberg and was a gift from the Peale family to the church. And another bronze life-size group sculpture, *The Flight into Egypt*, dedicated in 1966, was created by sculptor Anna Hyatt Huntington as a gift of Anna Hyatt Huntington to the church.

Norman Vincent Peale (1898–1993) was the pastor here from 1932 until he retired in 1984. He was an influential religious figure in America who pioneered the use of radio and television in his ministry and worked closely with Dr. Smiley Blanton, a psychiatrist trained by Sigmund Freud. Peale became one of the first ministers to bring psychological counseling to his congregation. But what made Peale famous more than anything else was the bestselling book he authored, *The Power of Positive Thinking*.

In 1870, the famous American actor Joseph Jefferson's friend, actor George Holland, died, and Jefferson went to the fashionable Marble Collegiate Church to arrange for funeral services. When the rector discovered that Holland was an actor, he politely declined and suggested that Jefferson go to the "little church around the corner," where the funeral services might be arranged. Jefferson was said to have responded, "Thank God for the little church around the corner." From then on, there has been a special connection between stage actors and the "Little Church Around the Corner." Sir Henry Irving, Dame Ellen Terry and Sarah Bernhardt attended services at this church. There are memorial windows in the church for some of America's most distinguished stage actors: Richard Mansfield, John Drew and Edwin Booth. Before going to the "Little Church Around the Corner," we should take a look at an office building that opened in 1929 on the southeast corner of Fifth Avenue and East 29th Street (261 Fifth Avenue), an Art Moderne gem with nice polychrome terra-cotta designs by architects Buckman & Kahn.

Now we will walk around the corner and take a look at **1 East 29th Street** between Fifth Avenue and Madison Avenue. It is the Episcopal church that is known by a few different names, among them the "Little Church Around the Corner" and the "Actors Chapel." It is, officially, the Church of the Transfiguration, built between 1849 and 1861. The architect is unknown. The Lych-gate was built in 1896, designed by architect Frederick C. Withers. The Lady Chapel was built in 1906 and the Mortuary Chapel in 1908, architects unknown. It is because of the diverse character of Murray Hill that when we come upon this ecclesiastical enclave resembling a picturesque English village church wedged between skyscrapers on the Manhattan grid, we are only mildly surprised. The enclave includes a brick and brownstone rectory that is a nice example of domestic Gothic Revival architecture, and it is a subsidiary part of the larger design that blends well with the adjacent church.

The church's main entrance is through the tower, which is supported by diagonally placed stepped buttresses and topped by a small peaked roof. At the tower's base and to its left are three arched windows of the Lady Chapel. To the right of the tower lies the main body of the church, divided unequally by squat buttresses. Above the nave are small dormers. St. Joseph's mortuary chapel is inside the octagonal crossing tower. The Lych-gate, unusual for an American churchyard, is supported by stone Gothic arches—it was intended to provide a covered resting place for the coffin before the burial service began. The Church of the Transfiguration is a New York City and a national landmark.

Now let's walk to Madison Avenue, and on the southeast corner, we'll see **89–95 East 29th Street**, the Emmet Building, built in 1912 and designed by J. Stewart Barney & Stockton B. Colt, associated architects, in an early French Neo-Renaissance style—terra cotta gone wild. The building was constructed by order of Dr. Thomas Emmet (1828–1919), an esteemed mid-nineteenth-century gynecologist who wrote the book *The Principles and Practices of Gynecology*. Emmet was the owner of and maintained an apartment on the top floor of the office building. His apartment included a solarium, a pergola, a roof garden, a library and a fountain. The 1915 census showed Dr. Thomas Emmet, eighty-seven years old and a widower, living there with his son, Thomas (fifty-one years old); Margaret O'Reilly, a nurse; and Koricki Myamiata, a cook. In 1919, Dr. Emmet died in his apartment here, and in 1920, the top floor was converted to commercial loft space. During his life, Dr. Emmet was an impassioned critic of English rule in Ireland. In 1803, his grand uncle, Robert Emmet, had been executed in Dublin by the English for starting an uprising. Dr. Emmet's remains were shipped to Dublin to be buried in his family's plot.

I wonder why this building is not a New York City landmark. Its façade is distinctively marked with terra-cotta sculpture of grotesque, medieval figures

Number 261 Fifth Avenue.

Church of the Transfiguration.

Emmet Building façade: carved limestone cavaliers and courtesans under terra-cotta canopies.

Number 88 Madison Avenue, East 29th Street entrance, Carlton Hotel (formerly Hotel Seville).

along with other elements, such as the rows of ornate pediment dormers pointing up out of the French Mansard roof. And below, over the first floor, are four carved limestone cavaliers and courtesans under terra-cotta canopies—two on Madison Avenue and two on the 29th Street façade, along with a second-floor cornice. And there are mischievous terra-cotta gargoyles with expressions of surprise and playfulness decorating both façades. The street-level floor exhibits a fusion of limestone, cast-iron ornamentation and green marble–clad pillars that are two stories in height. Although most of the details are early French Renaissance in style, the overall appearance of the building is superficially Gothic—much in the same way as the Woolworth Building. The building's façades were restored in 1991.

At the southwest corner of East 29th Street, **88 Madison Avenue** opened as the Hotel Seville in 1904, a Beaux Arts–style hotel designed by architect Harry Allen Jacobs with a rusticated limestone base and a red brick façade with white terra-cotta trim, rounded copper bays and sculptural ornaments such as cartouches and the panels with foliage and lion heads on the third floor—altogether a robust design.

Legend has it that as a teenager, Harpo Marx worked as a bellboy here and that several of the Marx brothers' skits were based on Harpo's experiences at Hotel Seville. And it is also rumored that the hotel had a speakeasy operating on the premises during prohibition. An even darker piece of Hotel Seville's history occurred in 1980 when a victim of the serial killer Richard Cottingham was found in the hotel. Cottingham, from New Jersey, killed people in New York between 1967 and 1980 and became nicknamed "the Torso Killer" because he dismembered his victims, leaving behind nothing but a torso. He was convicted of murder in 1981. Officially, Cottingham killed six people, but Cottingham bragged that he committed more than eighty-five murders.

In 1985, the hotel was purchased by new owners, who completely refurbished the guest rooms. In 1987, the hotel had a major upgrading, its façade was restored and it was renamed the Carlton Hotel on Madison Avenue. In 2003, the hotel's interior was modernized, refurbished and redesigned.

Number **121 Madison Avenue**, at the northeast corner of East 30th Street, opened in 1883 as the Hubert Home Club, co-operative apartments built and designed by Hubert Prisson & Company. That firm also built Hotel Chelsea at 222 West 23rd Street and the Rembrandt at 152 West 57th Street (demolished) as early co-operative apartment buildings in Manhattan. Originally, the Hubert Home Club was designed in Queen Ann style—twelve stories with five spacious duplexes on every two floors, each having a fireplace and entertaining rooms en suite via sliding mahogany glass etched doors. The building was altered and converted to rentals in 1917, losing some of its ornament. In 1940, the building endured a brutal alteration of its interior and exterior when it was converted into smaller rental apartments. The skyline suffered when they added a few stories on top. The building's cornice and decorative balconies were destroyed along with almost all of the façade decorations. At that time, the building's appearance was deteriorating, and all that it retained was a bulky look along with its red color and some remnants of its original architectural details. What goes around comes around, and if a building survives long enough, sometimes it can recoup some of the elegance of its past. This seems to be the case with 121 Madison because it was converted to spacious luxury rentals (high ceilings, designer granite kitchens and marble bathrooms). Throughout all of its changes, most apartments still retained their original fireplaces.

And now we'll walk north to **120 Madison Avenue**, the American Academy of Dramatic Arts, between East 30th Street and East 31st Street. The building was originally the Colony Club, built between 1904 and 1908 and designed by architect Stanford White of McKim, Mead & White in a combined Georgian–Federal Revival style. It was during the time the clubhouse was being constructed that its architect, Stanford White, was murdered by a jealous husband just three and a half blocks away. The façade has a grayish red brick and white limestone trim and features unusual brickwork with the headers (the short ends) facing out. The dominant feature of the façade's design are the five tall windows on its second floor set within recessed arches. There is a handsome stone cornice topped by a balustrade that separates the lower floors from the mansard roof and its dormers.

Originally, the interiors (many were given interior New York City landmark status) were designed by Elsie de Wolf for the socially prominent members of this private woman's club—the first private woman's club in New York to build its own clubhouse. Ann Morgan (J.P. Morgan's sister), Mrs. J. Borden Harriman and Helen Barney were founding members in 1901. It was a social club that sponsored good works, especially patronage of the arts. Elsie de Wolf, who later became "Lady Mendl," was a former actress who had opened an interior design business, and her companion was the theatrical agent Elisabeth Marbury, who also was one of the Colony Club's founders. The club moved in 1916 to a much larger clubhouse at Park Avenue and East 62nd Street.

The American Academy of Dramatic Arts moved into 120 Madison Avenue in 1963. The academy, founded in 1884, is the oldest school of

Number 120 Madison Avenue, the American Academy of Dramatic Arts (formerly the Colony Club).

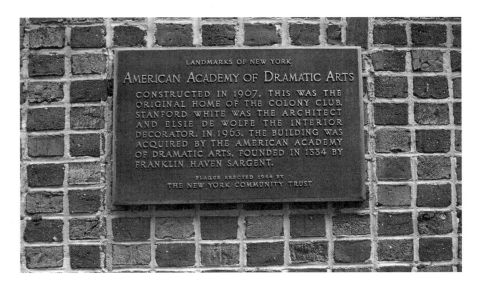

The Colony Club plaque.

professional dramatic training in the English-speaking world. A small sample of its alumni includes Spencer Tracy, Kirk Douglas, Lauren Bacall, Rosalind Russell, Edward G. Robinson, Ann Bancroft, Grace Kelly, Thelma Ritter, Robert Redford, Jennifer Jones, Dina Merrill, William Powell, Agnes Moorehead, Danny DeVito, Cecil B. DeMille and the list goes on and on.

Roger Williams Apartments was located at the southeast corner of Madison Avenue, at **28 East 31st Street**, in 1935. Author and painter Henry Miller (1891–1980) lived here for several months with Anais Nin while he finished *Black Spring*. They returned to France later in 1935. Miller's novels were banned in the United States and Britain on grounds of obscenity until the 1960s. Roger Williams Apartments was converted to Roger New York, a boutique hotel.

Originally, Roger Williams Apartments opened in 1930, designed by architectural firm Jardine, Hill & Murdock and named after the Baptist founder of Rhode Island, Roger Williams. In 1930, the Madison Avenue Baptist Church leased the property on Madison Avenue to be developed into a fifteen-story building, with the church's sanctuary to be included in the building, and it still is.

The Madison Avenue Baptist Church Parish House, at **30 East 31st Street**, was built in 1906 between Madison and Park Avenue and is a five-story, unconventional brick and limestone Romanesque Revival gem. Its spandrels are decorated with Middle Eastern motifs. On top is a copper cornice supported by unusually decorated brackets. The two strong elements of the parish house's design are the three-story-tall rounded arched openings, with recessed windows, and its ornate pedimented entrance.

The Rose Hill Baptist Church was organized in 1839. Its first sanctuary was at 154 Lexington Avenue (now the First Moravian Episcopal Church), and its second sanctuary, renamed the Madison Avenue Baptist Church, was built in 1858 at 133 Madison Avenue (site of Roger New York). The Madison Avenue Baptist Church offers the Sunday Afternoon Meal for Seniors (free meals for the Midtown elderly) and has a shelter for the homeless. The church has been offering ministries to persons with AIDS at Bellevue Hospital and is sponsored by the Bellevue Chaplain's Office. Madison Avenue Baptist Church is a charter member of the Association of Welcoming and Affirming Baptists, made up of American Baptist churches and organizations that want to include gays and lesbians.

If we walk back to Madison Avenue and to the southwest corner of East 32nd Street, we pass the Remsen Building, **148 Madison Avenue**. It was built in 1917 and altered in 1930; Frank Goodwillie was the architect. The base of

Numbers 158–152 Madison Avenue, Andy Warhol's former loft.

the building has moderate Art Moderne terra-cotta patterns and a distinctive Neo-Gothic entrance with hooded tripartite windows with finials.

Now looking across the street, we see at the northwest corner of East 32nd Street and **158 Madison Avenue** what was once a New York Edison substation, along with 19 East 32nd Street and 22 East 32nd Street; 158 Madison Avenue was remodeled in 1983. Andy Warhol (1928–1987) rented space in this building from 1980 to 1987 and used it for the Factory—a workshop and hangout for him and his entourage. This was the last of a series of locations in Manhattan that he used. Warhol was an American artist and a leading figure in the "pop art" visual art movement. His work examines relationships between artistic expression, celebrity culture and advertisement that flourished by the 1960s, and he became a renowned and sometimes controversial artist—more influential in the art world than his print of a Campbell soup can would suggest. Warhol died in New York Hospital after an operation on his gallbladder.

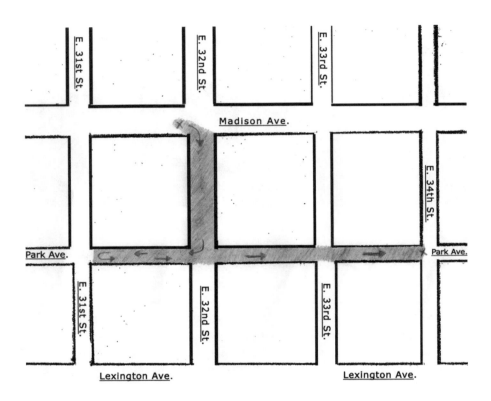

Chapter 10

OUR TOUR ENDS EXPRESSING A
MICROCOSM OF IDEAS AND HUMAN GOALS

*East 32nd Street, Park Avenue South, Park Avenue,
East 33rd Street and East 34th Street*

W e will walk on East 32nd Street toward Park Avenue and stop at **29 East 32nd Street**. It was built as the Grolier Club in 1889, designed by Charles W. Romeyn & Company in a highly original Romanesque Revival style. The three-story building denotes a feeling for its texture by the way the Roman brickwork is juxtaposed with the stonework. There are two large linked arches on the ground floor with handsome carvings that dominate the design. The second floor has a central rounded arch window flanked by narrow, high windows, and the three are connected by a slim molded sill at their base. The top floor has a row of four windows separated by columns.

The club was formed in 1884 for literary study and for the promotion of the publishing arts and derives its name from Jean Grolier, a sixteenth-century bibliophile. In 1917, the club relocated to 47 East 60th Street, and the building was converted to office space. At one time, the building was referred to as the Gilbert Kiamie House because the actor and dancer Gilbert Kiamie purchased the building in the 1940s and used it for his personal residence. After the ex-clubhouse was sold, it reverted back to office space again. Now it is called the Madison and is rented for special events. The Grolier Club is a New York City and a national landmark.

We now walk to the southwest corner of East 32nd Street and then toward East 31st to **462 Park Avenue South**. This is a Renaissance Revival, seventeen-story, hi-rise office building, the Schwarzenbach Building, also known as the Silk Center. It was built in 1912 and renovated in 1936. The building was named for Schwarzenbach Looms, makers of Darbrook Silks.

Number 29 East 32nd Street, Old Groliers Club.

Also see the Silk Clock hanging over the sidewalk between East 32nd Street and East 31st Street. The clock has moving figures that signal the hour, a blacksmith sits on top of the clock and the clock is surrounded by bas-relief leaves, caterpillars and butterflies. Above the clock is the Darbrook Silks Mosaic.

If we cross to the east side of Park Avenue South, we will see an outdoor sculpture in front of 475 Park Avenue South between East 31st Street and East 32nd Street. It is *Triad*, sculpted by Irving Marantz (1912–1972) in 1969, and it rests on a polished granite pedestal. The work is inspired by Picasso's *Three Musicians*, with its theme and cubistic arrangement of the elements. And the three figures may be a possible reference to the three Cohen brothers, the realtors who commissioned the work. The cluster of three abstract figures molded into planes and cubes emotes dignity from its pedestal.

Irving Marantz was a painter who worked as a sculptor only in the last five years of his life. *Triad* was his second major outdoor work as a sculptor. Marantz's last work is standing about two blocks north in front of **3 Park Avenue** near the southeast corner of East 34th Street: *Obelisk to Peace*, created in 1972 as an abstract representation of an ancient monumental form that

The Silk Clock, hanging at 475 Park Avenue South on the façade of the Schwarzenbach Building.

Outdoor sculpture *Triad* in front 475 Park Avenue South.

often glorified military victories. However, *Obelisk to Peace*'s organic shapes blend into one, suggesting unity and agreement. The twenty-three-foot-high golden-colored sculpture is easily noticed by passersby because of the brown brick building behind it, 475 Park Avenue South. East 32nd Street is where Park Avenue South ends and Park Avenue begins.

Before we get to *Obelisk to Peace*, we will pass by 2 Park Avenue, which is on the west side of Park Avenue between East 32nd Street and East 33rd Street. It was built between 1926 and 1928 and designed by architect Ely Jacques Kahn (1884–1972) of Buckman & Kahn in a bold Art Deco style (some call it Art Moderne). There is an orderly pier and spandrel pattern on the lower portion of the façade, but the upper floors explode into angular, terra-cotta Art Deco decorations in primary colors. The green, blue, black, yellow and red that burst from the geometric panels on the upper floor setbacks were created with colorist Leon V. Solon and form a layered tapestry with striking details. The ornamentations are dramatic and original, reflecting the design ideas that were exposed at the Arts Decoratifs of 1925 in Paris, France, along with the works of German Expressionists and a number of industrial designers.

The architect Ely Jacques Kahn had his office at 2 Park Avenue, and it was here in 1937 that Kahn allowed Ayn Rand to work in his office for about six months as an unpaid assistant while she was doing research for her book *The Fountainhead*.

On the very site where 2 Park Avenue is today, if we went back in time to 1878, we would see a grand opening for Alexander T. Stewart's Home for Women, a huge, seven-story cast-iron building designed by architect John Kellum with an ornate French Mansard roof and elaborate dormers and pinnacles. The entrance had three large, two-story-high, rounded arch openings flanked by columns and supporting an entablature. It occupied the entire block on the west side of Park Avenue between East 32nd Street and East 33rd Street. Stewart intended that his hotel be safe, morally upright and clean. The women should live in a comfortable and upscale environment despite their personal conditions. There was to be a library, common areas for conversation and casual pastimes, a communal dining room and pleasant rooms. Unfortunately, the home for women took more than twenty years to build (the Civil War and a depression). By the time it was completed, Alexander T. Stewart and architect Kellum had passed away. Stewart's widow, Cornelia, opened the women's home, but it soon was considered a failure—too much of a money loser. The women's home didn't attract enough women, probably because the rates were too high and the

Number 2 Park Avenue, Park Avenue Building.

restrictions were too harsh. Alexander T. Stewart's Home for Women closed, underwent interior alterations and reopened as the Park Avenue Hotel, which stood here until it was demolished in the mid-1920s and replaced by 2 Park Avenue in 1928.

At East 33rd Street and Park Avenue, there is an entrance to the tunnel that travels under Park Avenue and surfaces at East 40th Street (see chapter 1). This was the southern border of the Robert and Mary Lindley Murray's farm.

Finally, if we walk about a block toward East 34th Street, we will see **4 Park Avenue** on the west side of the avenue. It was built in 1912 as the Vanderbilt Hotel for Alfred Gwynne Vanderbilt (1877–1915), who was known as "the good-looking Vanderbilt." Alfred Vanderbilt was brought up in a palatial mansion on Fifth Avenue and West 58th Street along with two brothers and his sister, Gertrude, who married the boy across the street, Harry Payne Whitney, and became Gertrude Vanderbilt Whitney, the woman who founded the Whitney Museum, which is still with us today. Alfred Vanderbilt had the hotel built for permanent residents, a new generation of wealthy people who wanted freedom from household cares—including himself, as he had an apartment on the entire top two floors. Alfred G. Vanderbilt died a hero after giving his life jacket to a woman on the sinking *Lusitania* (a British

Number 4 Park Avenue, formerly Vanderbilt Hotel.

ship torpedoed by Germans off the coast of Ireland; 127 Americans died, and the incident contributed to the United States entering World War I).

The hotel was designed by Warren & Wetmore, which also designed Grand Central Terminal on East 42nd Street for the Vanderbilt family. The Vanderbilt Hotel's façade had delicate Adam-style terra-cotta decorations when it opened, but much of it has been removed over the decades, including statues on its parapet and especially the ornamentation on the lower floors that was composed of huge Adam-style windows with delicate fluted fans, colonnettes, helmets and lions heads, all mixed with a crisscross brick pattern.

On the interior, the ground floor had one huge lounge with high vaulted ceilings. A part of the ground floor was set up as a dining room, but there was a much larger grill room and bar, and the lower basement floor had several beautifully arched polychrome spaces decorated with terra cotta, ceramic walls and vaulted Guastavino tile ceilings. The hotel's amenities were many and included pneumatic tubes that delivered messages to and from all levels of the hotel in several seconds. Enrico Caruso (1873–1921), the famous opera star, lived at the Vanderbilt Hotel from 1920 to 1921; it was his last residence in America before he returned to Italy and died from pleurisy in August 1921. The Vanderbilt family sold the hotel in 1925, and by 1967, it had been converted into an apartment building.

Part of the old Vanderbilt Hotel interior is denoted a landmark, but the rest of the building is not—this raises interesting questions for preservationists. We can peek at the building's landmark interior by going to the northwest corner of East 33rd Street and Park Avenue. We are at the entrance to what is referred to by historians as the Dell Robbia Bar (also known as the Crypt) in the Vanderbilt Hotel. Now the hotel (4 Park Avenue) is an apartment house, but a restaurant presently occupies the space that was the Crypt. This room is a New York City landmark and is an outstanding example of a ceramic room, with its vaulted Guastavino tile ceiling merging with the ceramic tile walls. The ceramic tiles are decorated with flowers, faces and a variety of motifs. The Guastavino tiles are structural, textured and ivory colored. The ceramic tiles were created by the Rockwood Pottery Company in Cincinnati, a leading art pottery manufacturer of the day, while the Guastavino tiles were made by the Guastavino Fireproof Construction Company (the firm maintained offices in New York, Boston, Providence, Chicago and Milwaukee and had its manufacturing plant in Woburn, Massachusetts). In 1943, Rafael Guastavino Jr. sold the company to Malcolm S. Blodgett, who was the treasurer and Guastavino's business partner. The company's last project was in 1962.

The Subway Station at East 33rd Street and Park Avenue was part of New York City's first subway line and opened in 1904. The Interborough Rapid Transit (IRT) was designed by Heins & LaFarge and is a New York City landmark. The terra-cotta eagles that used to adorn the station were from the Seventy-first Regiment Armory, which opened on the site of 3 Park Avenue in 1905 (that is on the east side of Park Avenue between East 33rd Street and East 34th Street). They were placed at the subway station after the armory was replaced by 3 Park Avenue in 1976. I think that it was an appropriate visual remembrance of the armory, which opened above the subway only about a year after the subway station itself opened. There is a bronze plaque on the terrace wall of 3 Park Avenue on East 33rd Street that also commemorates the picturesque armory, which was designed by Clinton and Russell and used to occupy this site. The eagles are gone now, but you can still see remnants of the armory's foundation wall as you walk down the steps of the Park Avenue subway entrance. On your left, you will see a remnant of the armory's foundation wall—it's there as an unnoticed reminder of the city's past.

The first eleven stories of **3 Park Avenue** is the Norman Thomas High School for Commercial Education, and the rest is an office building, opened

The armory foundation's wall remnant at the Park Avenue subway entrance.

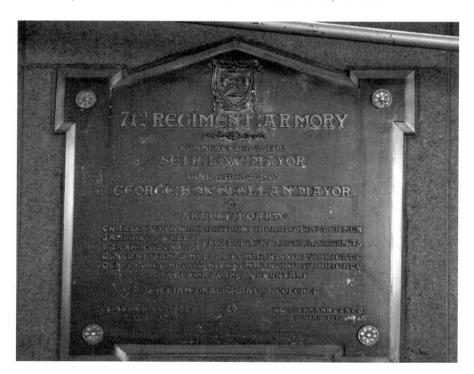

Seventy-first Regiment, armory plaque.

in 1976 and designed by architects Shreve Lamb & Harmon Associates. The firm created the forty-two-story sorrel brick tower that is placed diagonally to the city's street grid and the school, and it is highlighted at night when the top is flooded with orange light—quite the touch of Modernism.

In a way, this block is an appropriate place to end the walking tour of Murray Hill since the history represented on this Park Avenue block between East 34th Street and East 33rd Street can be seen as a microcosm of the diversity of Murray Hill's and the city's past. Consider that the school, named for Norman Thomas (1884–1968), is housed in a commercial skyscraper. Thomas was a founder of the American Socialist Party, a socialist, a pacifist and an American Presbyterian minister, and he ran for president of the United States six times as the candidate for the Socialist Party of America. The high school that bears his name is a school for commercial education, and the skyscraper that houses the school sits at an odd angle for New York City.

Also, this same building has the *Obelisk to Peace* sitting in front of it, and it features a plaque on its East 33rd Street wall commemorating an earlier building it replaced: the Seventy-first Regiment Armory for the New York State National Guard, which was built in 1905, replacing an earlier armory from 1894. The militia began as the American Rifles Militia, which was associated with the anti-immigrant Know-Nothing Party. In 1857, the unit quashed a Sixth Ward riot, killing the gang leader of the Dead Rabbits. In the Civil War, the militia fought at the First Battle of Bull Run and at Gettysburg, and in the Spanish-American War, it fought alongside the Rough Riders at the Battle of San Juan Hill. Now, there very well could be a connection between the militia and a yearning for peace, but there is also a wide variety of motives, ideas, ideologies and human goals that is represented by the plaque, by the obelisk, by the name Norman Thomas and by the school itself. Directly under the sidewalk here is the 33rd Street subway station, providing access to inexpensive transportation for Murray Hill's working class since 1904, and it sits below the old Vanderbilt Hotel, a remnant of the city's Gilded Age.

I hope that this tour leaves you with the idea that many very different ideas, ideologies and motives do not have to conflict but rather can exist together for a greater good—not one that is planned for, but one that evolves naturally from human differences. I believe that this is the story of New York City. Good luck, and I hope you enjoyed the tour.

BIBLIOGRAPHY

Alpern, Andrew. *Luxury Apartment Houses of Manhattan: An Illustrated History*. Mineola, NY: Dover Publications, 1912.

Burrows, Edwin G., and Mike Wallace. *Gotham: A History of New York City to 1898*. New York: Oxford University Press, 1999.

Chernow, Ron. *The House of Morgan*. A Touchtone Book. New York: Simon & Schuster, 1991.

Diamondstein, Barbaralee. *The Landmarks of New York*. Vol. 2. New York: Harry N. Abrams Inc., 1993.

Dolkhart, Andrew S., and Matthew A. Postal. *Guide to New York City Landmarks*. 4th ed. Edited by Matthew A. Postan. New York City Landmarks Preservation Commission. Hoboken, NJ: John Wiley & Sons, 2009.

Dunlap, David W., and Joseph J. Vecchione. *Glory in Gotham: Manhattan Houses of Worship, a Guide to Their History, Architecture and Legacy*. New York: City & Company, 2001.

Ellis, Edward Robb. *The Epic of New York City*. New York: Old Town Books, 1990.

Gale, Margot, and Michele Cohen. *The Art Commission and the Municipal Art Society Guide to Manhattan's Outdoor Sculpture*. New York: Prentice Hall Press, 1988.

Goldsmith, Barbara. *Other Powers: The Age of Suffrage, Spiritualism, and the Scandalous Victoria Woodhull*. New York: HarperCollins Publishers, 1999.

Gray, Christopher. *New York Streetscapes: Tales of Manhattan's Significant Buildings and Landmarks*. New York: Abrams, 2003.

Homberger, Eric. *Mrs. Astor's New York: Money and Social Power in a Gilded Age*. New Haven, CT: Yale University Press, 2002.

Monaghan, Charles. *The Murrays of Murray Hill*. 1st ed. Brooklyn, NY: Urban History Press, 1998.

Nolan, William F. *Hammett: A Life at the Edge*. New York: Congdon & Weed Inc., 1983.

Patterson, Jerry E. *The First Four Hundred: Mrs. Astor's New York in the Gilded Age*. New York: Rizzoli International Publications Inc., 2000.

Reynolds, Donald M. *The Architecture of New York City*. New York: Macmillan Publishers, 1983.

Shaver, Peter D., comp. *The National Register of Historic Places in New York State*. Compiled for the Preservation League of New York State. New York: Rizzoli International Publications Inc., 1993.

White, Norval, and Elliot Willensky, with Fran Leadon. *AIA Guide to New York City*. 5th ed. New York: Oxford University Press, 2010.

Index

ABOUT THE AUTHORS

ALFRED POMMER of New York City Cultural Walking Tours is a self-employed, licensed New York City guide. He has been giving private and publicly scheduled neighborhood walking tours for groups or individuals in Manhattan's many diverse neighborhoods for more than twenty-three years. During that time, Alfred has been constantly researching and improving each tour. He retired in 1991 after twenty-five years of service with the New York City Parks Department. During that time, he attended college part time, eventually graduating Empire College (SUNY) with a Bachelor of Science degree in labor studies. Alfred has authored two previous guidebooks, *Exploring New York's SoHo* and *Exploring the Original West Village*, in collaboration with Eleanor Winters and published by The History Press. He has also had several articles published by *10003 Magazine* about the history of various locations, streets and neighborhoods in Manhattan.

www.nycwalk.com

JOYCE POMMER is an abstract mixed-media artist and independent curator. Having owned a gallery in Manhattan for eight years, as director she wrote press releases and artist synopses. Now she has returned to focus on her own painting and is reemerging as Joyce Pommer + Projects. Originally from Boston, Joyce studied at the Academy of Art College in San Francisco, the Art Institute of Boston and the Art Students League in New York City.

She has exhibited in numerous solo and group shows in New York City and across the country, and her works are included in numerous private collections. She maintains a studio in the garment district in Manhattan.

Joyce also works as a nurse consultant for a law firm, editing medical records and writing case reports. This is her first venture in coauthoring with her husband, Alfred.

www.joycepommer.com